Santa Walks Into a Bar...

And Other Hilarious Christmas Jokes and Stories

Santa Walks Into a Bar...

And Other Hilarious Christmas Jokes and Stories

Roger Johnson

FOLK
LORE
PUBLISHING

©2013 by Folklore Publishing
First printed in 2013 10 9 8 7 6 5 4 3 2 1
Printed in Canada

All rights reserved. No part of this work covered by the copyrights hereon may be reproduced or used in any form or by any means—graphic, electronic or mechanical—without the prior written permission of the publisher, except for reviewers, who may quote brief passages. Any request for photocopying, recording, taping or storage on information retrieval systems of any part of this work shall be directed in writing to the publisher. .

The Publisher: Folklore Publishing
Website: www.folklorepublishing.com

Library and Archives Canada Cataloguing in Publication

Johnson, Roger, 1977–, author
    Santa walks into a bar : Christmas jokes with an edge
/ Roger Johnson.

ISBN 978-1-926677-90-3 (pbk.)

    1. Christmas—Humor. I. Title.

PN6231.C36J63 2013   C818'.602   C2013-905457-X

Project Director: Faye Boer
Project Editor: Sheila Quinlan
Cover Images: Santa © Dennis Cox / Photos.com; elf © Igor Zakowski / Photos.com; reindeer © Diego Mera / Photos.com; night sky background © Neven Bijelic / Photos.com

Produced with the assistance of the Government of Alberta, Alberta Multimedia Development Fund.

We acknowledge the financial support of the Government of Canada through the Canada Book Fund (CBF) for our publishing activities.

 Canadian Heritage   Patrimoine canadien

PC: 24

✎ CONTENTS ❧

The Untold, True History of Santa Claus

1689: Spanish-German explorer Santa Claus, age 25, discovers the North Pole and establishes a small base camp.

1691: Because of harsh and meager living conditions, Claus' crew abandons him.

1692: Claus is rescued by the Norse ship *Hvorfor*. He returns to Europe, bringing some items along with him from the North Pole. He finds he is able to sell them quite easily, making a small profit.

1703: Claus saves up enough money to buy a small ship and hire a crew, and returns to the North Pole. Upon arriving, he finds his base camp half-buried but still intact.

1704: Claus returns to Europe with a shipload of North Pole artifacts and is successful in selling them. He makes enough profit to increase his crew and buys building materials to expand his polar base.

1705: Claus returns again to the North Pole and builds quarters for himself and his crew, and sets up the Polar Exports Company.

1716: After six shiploads of exports, the European market is flooded with polar artifacts, as well as the phony ones making charlatans rich. Seeing this decline, Claus decides to invest his money by starting a toy company in his native Germany.

1720: Claus Toys becomes the largest toy company in Germany, but only because of Claus' underhanded business dealings. (It was rumored that Claus was dealing with enemy countries as well.) Competitors urged government officials to begin an investigation.

1721: Enough evidence is found, and charges are drawn up against Claus Toys. Claus refuses to release his records.

1722: The German Supreme Court finds Claus guilty of tax evasion and treason. When news of the verdict breaks, Claus' employees all turn against him and his company.

1723: Claus is exiled to Sicily, and he absconds with all of the company's funds.

1724: A search party is sent to the Mediterranean to recover the funds; however, Claus hears of this ahead of time, and he and his Sicilian wife flee for their lives. They head for the North Pole.

1725: Santa Claus II is born en route to the North Pole.

1725–1734: The Clauses lay low at the North Pole. Claus teaches his son the arts of toy making and business dealings.

1735: Claus hires Scandinavian builders to construct a castle for him at the North Pole, making use of almost half of the remaining company funds.

1740: The castle is finished, and it is one of the largest in the world. Claus II reaches his 15th birthday, and later that year Claus' wife dies, accidentally falling from a balcony in the castle's great hall.

1741: Claus, mourning his wife, becomes a recluse. His health starts to decline.

1746: Claus II comes of age and begins taking care of the castle and his sick father.

1747: Using the remaining company funds, Claus II begins to build a small city around the castle to attract workers and craftsmen.

1748: Word of the North Pole settlement reaches Europe. The Elves of Eastern Europe, quickly becoming political outcasts and striving for a better life, begin immigrating in waves to the North Pole.

1754: The Elves have become firmly established at the North Pole. Claus II reestablishes his father's toy company, with an estimated 30,000 Elves employed. Claus I, now 90 years old, dies after one final battle with pneumonia.

1756: The North Pole officially becomes a nation, and Claus II and his wife take the throne. The toy business continues to flourish, and the elves enjoy prosperity. Santa Claus III is born.

1757: The great stables are built, and Claus II secretly hires scientists to begin an ambitious project—that of breeding and training reindeer to fly.

1773: The flying reindeer are achieved and become the Clauses' major form of transportation.

1775: A mutant reindeer whose nose emits light, named Rudolph, is born. He becomes an outcast of the reindeer society and is taken in by the Claus government. Claus II celebrates his 50th birthday, inviting several other world leaders for a stay at his castle. To impress them, he displays a lavish show of wealth, all at the Elves' expense. He gives the other leaders the impression of a dictatorship under the guise of a monarchy. The Elves sense this shift, and the seeds of rebellion are planted.

1777: As conditions become increasingly strict, the Elves begin to search for a leader to lead their revolt. Rudolph, still in favor with the Claus government, sees the Elves' plight and begins thinking of ways to use it to his advantage.

1785: On his 60th birthday, Claus II takes a sleigh ride down Main Street during the Christmas Day parade and is assassinated by a radical faction of Elves. Claus III, now 29, takes over immediately and puts martial law into effect for the whole North Pole. Civil war breaks out as Rudolph leads the Elves in rebellion.

1786–1793: The Seven-year Strike takes place. The Elves refuse to make toys, and the Claus Toy Company nearly goes bankrupt as the North Pole hits an economic low. Claus III, fearing for his life, becomes a prisoner in his own castle. Rudolph rises to the peak of his power and establishes himself as leader of the Elven community.

1796: Rudolph and his army unsuccessfully attempt to invade Norway. Over 10,000 Elves are killed.

1800: Inside the castle, unbeknownst to the Elves, Santa Claus IV is born.

1802: After a string of political blunders, Rudolph senses that he is quickly losing favor with the Elves. Frosty the Snowman is built, brought to life and used as a political scapegoat.

1804: Frosty the Snowman is melted at a public execution. Just before his head melted Frosty threatened to come back again someday, but the Elves are calmed of their unrest, for the moment.

1826: After a long period of renewed unrest, Rudolph is finally ousted, and Claus III, aged 70, rightfully regains the throne. Prince Claus IV is introduced to the Elves publicly for the first time.

1827–1841: The Renormalization Years. Claus III brings the near-bankrupt Claus Toys out of dormancy and appoints his son as president. In order to clear their bad name and make up for their out-of-the-way location, they decide to start the hugest advertising campaign ever. Each Christmas, Claus IV will ride all over the world, distributing free toys to children everywhere. The ad campaign becomes a hit but is very costly.

1837: Claus III dies at age 81.

1851: As the annual ad campaign continues, deficits pile up. The Elves are asked to work harder, longer hours and still take a pay cut. They start to complain, but Claus IV assures them he will do all he can to help them. As a sign of goodwill, Claus IV marries an Elven wife, strengthening the bonds between the Claus family and the Elves.

1856: Santa Claus V is born. In order to celebrate and bond with his son, Claus IV decides to stay at home in the lead-up to Christmas, and he suggests that department stores use costumed employees to represent him. They do, and it works out so well that he decides to do it every year.

1857–1867: Claus V grows up spending most of his time visiting with his Elf relatives and friends. Claus IV, who spends most of his time building up the company, doesn't seem to mind; in fact, he feels that it's good public relations.

1871: Working conditions have continued to worsen for the Elves, and they try to convince Claus V to overthrow his father and give the government back to the elves.

1874: Claus V usurps his father's throne, sending him to live the remainder of his life under guard in the castle's west wing.

1875: After reading the works of Karl Marx, Claus V chooses communism as the new form of government for the North Pole. Some Elves protest, but they are successfully quieted. (It is because of communism that Santa Claus' suit changes from beige to red.)

1883: Claus IV dies in captivity. His funeral is not a large one.

1887: To keep up with growing populations, Claus Toys becomes industrialized. The Elves learn the ways of mass production on the assembly line.

1893: Another mutant reindeer is born and is named Rudolph II in honor of the first one, whom the communist government now honors for "giving the government back to the Elves."

1902: After he had been presumed dead for years, Frosty the Snowman is claimed to have been sighted on several occasions.

1905: Santa Claus VI is born. The Claus family celebrates, but the Elves aren't the least bit excited.

1909–1922: The toys distributed yearly begin to show signs of propaganda influence. Frosty the Snowman continues to appear occasionally, and Claus V begins to grow uneasy, fearing some sort of hidden sabotage.

1925: Claus V dies under mysterious circumstances. He is found buried in the snow in the castle garden, frozen solid. Many think it is the work of Frosty, but no one can prove it.

1926: Claus VI, now 21, takes over and immediately tightens up security. He rules with an iron hand, but a fair one. The castle and the town get electricity. The factories are expanded, and the toys continue to be used as propaganda for the world.

1929: Angered by Claus' commercialization of Christmas, the Grinch attempts to remove the material goods to show the true meaning of Christmas. He fails, and later Claus commissions a book that warps the story so that the Grinch is made out to be the villain.

1949: Santa Claus VII is born.

1979: Claus VI dies of natural causes.

1933–1990: The North Pole remains stable, with everything running smoothly. Across the Western world, a pattern starts to emerge and become noticed. Children receive Claus' toys each Christmas, but as they grow older, their parents throw them away. When they have children of their own, they are surprised to see the toys once again. And so the cycle goes on.

1991: First sightings of Anti-Claus.

1993: Anti-Claus is observed closely with telescopes, and photographed. His suit is like that of Santa Claus, but with the red and white reversed. He carries a 3-ply Hefty bag full of gifts no one wants or needs. And instead of using reindeer and a sleigh, he rides in a bathtub pulled by eight flying cows.

1997: Anti-Claus is radar-tracked·and found to live in an underground hideout run by Dwarves at the South Pole.

2002: Communism fails utterly at the North Pole due to the nature of the Elves. Claus VII, flying clockwise around the earth making the Christmas rounds, collides with Anti-Claus, who was flying counterclockwise. A huge explosion occurs, leading scientists to believe that they annihilated each other.

2007: The North Pole is now a democracy, run wholly by the Elves. Christmas is no longer commercialized or exploited. Happiness is finally achieved throughout the country.

2011: It is discovered that Claus VII did not die in the explosion, but merely made it appear so.

2013: Claus VII returns to the North Pole to overthrow the Elf democracy. Christmas might not happen...

CHAPTER ONE

Santa and Mrs. Claus

Santa walks into a bar...

After years of living at the North Pole and being away from modern society, Santa walks into a bar in a big city and orders a drink. He tells the bartender to send two drinks to the two attractive women he sees sitting at the other end of the bar.

"Take my advice," says the bartender. "Don't waste your money on those two; they're lesbians."

"That doesn't bother me," says Santa. "Send the two lovely ladies each a drink on me."

A while later, Santa orders another drink and tells the bartender to send two more to the women at the end of the bar.

"Okay," says the bartender, "but I'm telling you, you're wasting your time. They're both lesbians."

Finally, Santa decides to make his move. He sits down next to the two women and strikes up a conversation. "I understand you ladies are both lesbians," he says.

"That's right," replies one of the women.

"You know, I've led a sheltered life way up in the North Pole surrounded by my wife and all the elves. Can you tell me exactly what a lesbian is?"

"Sure," says the other lesbian. "We like big, big boobs, and we just love having lots of sex when we get together with friends."

"Wow! That sounds great to me!" says Santa. "Bartender, another round of drinks over here for us lesbians."

A Tradition

One particular Christmas season a long time ago, Santa was getting ready for is annual trip, but there were problems everywhere. Four of his elves got sick, and the trainee elves did not produce the toys as fast as the regular ones, so Santa was beginning to feel the pressure of being behind schedule. Then Mrs. Claus told Santa that her mom was coming to visit. This stressed out Santa even more.

Q: Why does Santa wear pink underwear?

A: He's a man. He did all his laundry in one load.

When he went to harness the reindeer on Christmas Eve, he found that three of them were about to become parents and two had jumped the fence and were out, heaven knows where. More stress.

Then when he began to load the sleigh, one of the boards cracked and the toy bag fell to the ground and scattered the toys. So, frustrated, Santa went into the house for a cup of apple cider and a shot of rum.

When he went to the cupboard, he discovered that Mrs. Claus had hidden the liquor. In his frustration, he accidentally dropped the cider pot, and it broke into hundreds of little pieces all over the kitchen floor. He went to get the broom and found that mice had eaten the straw end of the broom.

Just then the doorbell rang, and irritable Santa trudged to the door. He opened it, and there was a little angel with a great big Christmas tree.

The angel said, very cheerfully, "Merry Christmas, Santa. Isn't it a lovely day? I have a beautiful tree for you. Where would you like me to stick it?"

Thus began the tradition of the little angel on top of the Christmas tree.

Santa's Pick-up Lines

- I know when you've been bad or good—so let's skip the small talk, sister!
- Hey babe, when was the last time you did it in a sleigh?
- Ever make it with a fat guy with a whip?
- Some of my best toys run on batteries. <wink wink>
- I see you when you're sleeping—you don't wear any underwear, do you?
- Screw the "nice" list—I've got you on my "nice AND naughty" list.
- Wanna join the mile high club?
- That's not a candy cane in my pocket, honey—I'm just glad to see you.

Do You Know Santa's True Profession?

Consider the following:

1. You never actually see Santa, only his "assistants."

2. Santa keeps his job until he decides to retire.

3. Santa doesn't really do the work; he directs a bunch of helpers to do all his work for him, but he's the one who everybody credits with the work.

4. Santa doesn't work anywhere near a 40-hour week.

5. Santa travels a lot.

Santa is obviously a senior faculty member with tenure!

Naughty Claus

A beautiful and amorous Santa groupie decides she is going to give Santa a present he won't forget. So she puts on a negligee, sheer panties and a robe and sits next to the fireplace on Christmas Eve.

Around midnight, Santa drops down the chimney and places some presents under the tree. He is about to leave when the young woman says in her sexiest voice, "Oh Santa, please stay. Help me keep the chill away."

Santa replies, "HO HO HO! Gotta go, gotta go! Gotta get the presents to the children, you know."

The woman drops her robe to reveal the see-through nightie and pleads, "Oh Santa, don't go so soon. Let's go to the couch and spoon."

Santa, feeling flushed, replies, "HO HO HO! Gotta go, gotta go! Gotta get the presents to the children, you know."

The woman takes off her top and says, "Oh, Santa, please stay. Help me celebrate Christmas Day."

Santa's eyes get wide, but still he answers, "HO HO HO! Gotta go, gotta go! Gotta get the presents to the children, you know."

Finally, she slips off her panties, winks at him, and says, "Oh, Santa...please..."

With a smile, Santa says, "HEY HEY HEY! Gotta stay, gotta stay! Can't get up the chimney with my pecker this way."

Release

After another Christmas and a year of hard work, Santa is tired of the same routines. So, finishing up a little early, he decides to try something new before going home to Mrs. Claus by visiting a whorehouse where the naughtiest girls worked. Santa has been with a few naughty girls before, but he wants to try the naughtiest.

Santa walks into the house and says to the madam, "I want a partner who will come up with something that I have never tried or heard about, and trust me, I've been around a long time."

"You will be very happy with Sadie then," says the madam. "If you're looking for something really new and different, try a wink job with her."

Not knowing what a wink job is, Santa goes up to the fourth-floor room and meets Sadie. To his disgust she is old, ugly and, what's more, she's got a glass eye. Before he can magically disappear, Sadie pulls out the eye and invites him to plant his love muscle into the empty hole in her face. He does, and then she winks and winks away, until he experiences a thrill like none of the naughty girls could ever do for him before.

"That was incredible, Sadie," says Santa. "I'll be back again next year for one of those wink jobs."

"Any time, big boy," she says. "I'll be keeping an eye out for ya."

Drunk Santa Before Christmas

'Twas the night before Christmas,
Old Santa was p*ssed;
He cussed out the elves
And threw down his list.

"Miserable little brats,
Ungrateful little jerks.
I have a good mind
To scrap the whole works!

I've busted my ass
For damn near a year;
Instead of 'Thanks, Santa,'
What do I hear?

The old lady bitched
'Cause I work late at night.
The elves want more money;
The reindeer all fight.

And just when I thought
That things would get better,
Those a**holes from the IRS
Sent me a letter.

They say I owe taxes—
If that ain't damn funny—
Who the hell ever
Sent Santa Claus money?

And the kids these days—
They all are the pits;
They want the impossible,
Those mean little sh*ts.

I spent a whole year
Making wagons and sleds,
Assembling dolls—
Their arms, legs and heads.

I made a ton of yo-yos—
No request for them;
They want computers and robots.
They think I'm IBM!

Flying through the air,
Dodging the trees,
Falling down chimneys
And skinning my knees—

I'm quitting this job;
There's just no enjoyment.
I'll sit on my fat ass
And draw unemployment.

There's no Christmas this year;
Now you know the reason.
I found me a blonde.
I'm going SOUTH for the season!"

Cocky Santa

Santa is alone at a fancy restaurant. He notices a beautiful woman sitting all alone at a table in the corner. He decides to send her a bottle of wine to get her attention. Santa tells the busboy to give her a bottle of their most expensive wine and tell her it's from him.

The busboy does as instructed and returns with a note from the woman. The note reads, "For me to accept this bottle, you must have a Mercedes in the driveway, one million dollars in the bank, and seven inches in your pants."

Santa sends the woman a note back. His note reads, "For your information, I am Santa Claus and I can have anything I want, and not even for a woman as beautiful as you would I cut three inches off my penis. Just send the bottle back."

Division of Labor

Dear children of the Southern United States:

I regret to inform you that, effective immediately, I will no longer be able to serve the Southern United States on Christmas Eve. Due to the overwhelming current population of the world, my contract was renegotiated by North American Fairies and Elves Local 209. I now serve only certain areas of Ohio, Indiana, Illinois, Wisconsin and Michigan. As part of the new and better contract, I also get longer breaks for milk and cookies. However, I'm certain that your children will be in good hands with your local replacement, who happens to be my third cousin, Bubba Claus. His side of the family is from the South Pole. He shares my goal of delivering toys to all the good boys and girls; however, there are a few differences between us.

1. There is no danger of a Grinch stealing your presents from Bubba Claus. He has a gun rack on his sleigh and bumper sticker that reads, "These toys insured by Smith and Wesson."

2. Instead of milk and cookies, Bubba Claus prefers that children leave an RC cola and pork rinds or a moon pie on the fireplace. And Bubba doesn't smoke a pipe. He dips a little snuff though, so please have an empty spit can handy.

3. Bubba Claus' sleigh is pulled by floppy-eared, flying coon dogs instead of reindeer. I made the mistake of loaning him a couple of my

reindeer one time, and Blitzen's head now overlooks Bubba's fireplace.

4. You won't hear "On Dasher, on Dancer, on Prancer and Vixen..." when Bubba Claus arrives. Instead, you'll hear, "On Earnhardt, on Wallace, on Martin and Labonte; on Rudd, on Jarrett, on Elliott and Petty."

5. "Ho, ho, ho!" has been replaced by "Yee-haw!"

6. As required by Southern highway laws, Bubba Claus' sleigh does have a Yosemite Sam safety triangle on the back with the words "Back Off!" The last I heard, the back of the sleigh had other decorations as well. One is a Ford logo with lights that race through the letters and the other is a caricature of me (Santa Claus) going wee on the Tooth Fairy.

7. The usual Christmas movie classics such as *Miracle on 34th Street* and *It's a Wonderful Life* will not be shown in your negotiated viewing area. Instead, you'll see *Boss Hogg Saves Christmas* and *Smokey and the Bandit IV*, featuring Burt Reynolds as Bubba Claus and dozens of state patrol cars crashing into each other.

8. Bubba Claus doesn't wear a belt. If I were you, I'd make sure you, the wife and the kids turn the other way when he bends over to put presents under the tree.

9. And finally, rather than lovely Christmas songs sung about me like "Santa Claus is Coming to Town," songs about Bubba Claus will be played on all the AM radio stations in

the South. Those song titles will include Mark Chesnutt's "Bubba Claus Shot the Jukebox," Cledus T. Judd's "All I Want for Christmas Is My Woman and a Six Pack," and Hank Williams Jr.'s "If You Don't Like Bubba Claus, You Can Shove It."

Sincerely yours,

Santa Claus

Computer Aid

Mrs. Claus is helping her computer-illiterate husband set up his new computer so he can more easily update his naughty and nice list. At the appropriate point in the process, she tells him that he will need to choose and enter a password to log on.

Santa is in a rather amorous mood and figures he will try for the shock effect. So when the computer asks him to enter his password, he makes it plainly obvious to Mrs. Claus that he is keying in p-e-n-i-s.

Q: Do you know why Santa doesn't have any children?

A: He only comes once a year, and that's down a chimney.

Mrs. Claus falls off her chair laughing when the computer replies: "Password rejected. Not long enough."

Top 10 Ways to Annoy Santa

10. Instead of milk and cookies, leave him a salad and a note explaining that you think he could stand to lose a few pounds.

9. While he's in the house, go find his sleigh and write him a speeding ticket.

8. Leave him a note explaining that you've gone away for the holidays. Ask if he would mind watering your plants.

7. While he's in the house, replace all his reindeer with replicas. Then wait and see what happens when he tries to get them to fly.

6. Keep an angry bull in your living room. If you think a bull goes crazy when he sees a little red cape, wait until he sees that big red Santa suit!

5. Build an army of mean-looking snowmen on the roof, holding signs that say, "We hate Christmas," and, "Go away, Santa."

4. Leave a note by the telephone telling Santa that Mrs. Claus called and wanted to remind him to pick up some milk and a loaf of bread on his way home.

3. Keep the fire burning hot and intense.

2. Leave Santa a bottle of beard moisturizer that you've emptied and refilled with hair removal cream.

1. Lace the carrots you leave for the reindeer with laxatives.

Santa Sued

From the law offices of Everey, Crooke and Fellon:

Due to numerous suits pending against our client, Mr. Santa Claus regrettably will not be available to present gifts or make any appearances in this Yuletide season. The office of Mr. Claus has, however, issued the following brief statement.

This document, hereafter named "the Christmas wish," is a Christmas statement of profoundly felt best wishes from Mr. Santa Claus, Esq., hereafter named "the party in the first," to Mr. Thomas Magliozzi and Mr. Raymond Magliozzi, the wishees, hereafter named "the party in the second." The conditions described in this Christmas wish pertain only to the current situation and must not be misinterpreted, misconstrued, perverted or falsified in any way whatsoever, by whomsoever, whensoever, wheresoever. The declaration of best wishes does not and must not be assumed to mean that the party in the first will act in any activities, either solely or in cahoots with other parties, either overtly or surreptitiously, in any way whatsoever, by means of the giving of gifts or the proffering of any acts of devotion, to attempt to grant the aforementioned wishes or to achieve fulfillment of the aforementioned wishes.

This letter also serves to inform the party in the second that the party in the first is bestowing a wish of prosperity and happiness for Christmas and the coming year. The good tidings furnished by the party in the first are not transferable to any subsequent year, and certainly cannot be considered retrospec-tively for any other occasions, either Christmases or otherwise, in times bygone, and must not, under any circumstances, be redeemed for cash. This wish is not to be misunderstood as an avowed guarantee that the party in the second will have a happy Christmas or prosperous New Year, and the party in the first is hereby indemnified from any legal recourse that the party in the second may wish to pursue if said party fails to have a happy Yuletide.

Thank you.

Hot Daughters

Santa Claus is sitting at home on December 26, resting after a busy season. He is sitting by the fire, warming his feet and talking with his four incredibly hot daughters, when suddenly there is a knock at the door. It is a young man who announces,

"My name is Lance,
And I'd like the chance
To go to the dance
With your daughter Nance."

Santa agrees and lets his daughter leave. Moments later, another guy shows up and says,

"My name is Joe,
And I'd like to go
To the picture show
With your daughter Flo."

Santa gives his permission. Moments later, another young man comes in and says,

"My name is Teddy,
And I'm really ready
To eat some spaghetti
With your daughter Betty."

Off Teddy and Betty go to eat. About an hour later there's a long knocking on the door. Father Christmas opens it and in staggers a drunk young man who begins to slur,

"My name is Tucker…"

Tucker never got a Christmas gift again.

Santa walks into a bar…again…

Santa walks into a bar with a magical dog and sits him on a stool beside him. Santa orders a beer, and when the bartender brings it to him, he says, "I'll bet you the price of this beer that my dog Jim here can talk."

"You're on!" says the bartender.

"Okay, watch this," Santa says. He stares the dog in the eye, points at the ceiling and says, "What's up there, boy?"

"Wroof! Wroof!" replies the dog.

"See," says Santa. "He called it a roof—this beer is on the house!"

"You've got to be joking. Of course Santa Claus's dog knows how to say roof," says the bartender. "You conned me. Pay up."

"No, wait," says Santa. "This time you ask him a question. Go on, ask Jim anything you want."

"Okay," says the bartender, "but if he doesn't speak clearly, you're paying for the next beer." The bartender stares the dog straight in the eye and says, "Who is the greatest hockey player of all time?"

The dog looks like he is thinking a moment, then looks up at the bartender and lets out a loud, "Howwwww, Howwwww, Howwww!"

"See, he got it right again," says Santa. "He said, 'Howe,' and Gordie Howe was the greatest hockey player of all time. I win the bet! Give me another free beer."

"That's it," says the bartender. "I've had enough of you. Get the hell out of my bar NOW!" The bartender grabs Santa and the dog and tosses them out the door onto the sidewalk.

Santa is lying on his back in the gutter when Jim walks over to him, licks his face and says, "Sorry about that. I knew I should have said Wayne Gretzky!"

Factory Tour

One year, Santa decides to go on a tour of several factories to get ideas for how to make his workshop more efficient. One factory produces various latex products. At the first stop on the assembly line, he is shown the machine that manufactures baby bottle nipples. The machine makes a loud *hiss-pop* noise. "The hiss is the rubber being injected into the mold," explains the guide. "The popping sound is the needle poking a hole in the end of the nipple."

Later, the tour reaches the part of the factory where condoms are manufactured. The machine makes a *hiss-hiss-hiss-hiss-pop* noise.

"Wait a minute!" says Santa. "I understand what the hissing is, but what's that pop every so often?"

"Oh, it's just the same as in the bottle nipple machine," says the guide. "It pokes a hole in every fifth condom."

"Well, that can't be good for the condoms!"

"Yeah, but it's great for the baby bottle nipple business."

Santa the Pr*ck

'Twas the night before Christmas,
And all through the house,
Not a creature was stirring,
Not even the mouse.

With Mom standing on the corner,
And Dad out with a lass,
I'd just settled down
With a young piece of ass.

When out on the lawn,
There arose such a clatter,
I sprang from my bed
To see what was the matter.

Then out on the lawn
I saw the pr*ck.
I knew at that moment
It must be St. Nick.

He came down the chimney
Like a bat out of hell.
I knew in that moment
The f*cker had fell.

With pretzels and beer
He filled up my stocking
And gave a big rubber d*ck
To my sister for cocking.

He rose up the chimney
With a thunderous fart.
The son of a b*tch
Blew the chimney apart.

Santa Must Be a Woman:
An Argument from a Woman's Point of View

I think Santa Claus is a woman. I hate to be the one to defy sacred myth, but I believe he's a she. Think about it. Christmas is a big, organized, warm, fuzzy, nurturing social deal, and I have a tough time believing a guy could possibly pull it all off.

For starters, the vast majority of men don't even think about selecting gifts until Christmas Eve. It's as if they are all frozen in some kind of Ebenezerian Time Warp until 3:00 pm on December 24, when they—with amazing calm—call other errant men and plan for a last-minute shopping spree. Once at the mall, they always seem surprised to find only Ronco products, socket wrench sets and mood rings left on the shelves. You might think this would send them into a fit of panic and guilt, but my husband tells me it's an enormous relief because it lessens the 11th-hour decision-making burden. On this count alone, I'm convinced Santa is a woman. Surely, if he were a man, everyone in the universe would wake up Christmas morning to find a rotating, musical Chia Pet under the tree, still in the bag from the store.

Another problem for a he-Santa would be getting there. First of all, there would be no reindeer because they would all be dead, gutted and strapped onto the rear bumper of the sleigh amid wide-eyed, desperate claims that buck season had been extended. Blitzen's rack would already be on the way to the taxidermist.

Even if the male Santa did have reindeer, he'd still have transportation problems because he would inevitably get lost up there in the snow and clouds and then refuse to stop and ask for directions. Add to this the fact that there would be unavoidable delays in the chimney, where the Bob Vila–like Santa would stop to inspect and repoint bricks in the flue. He would also need to check for carbon monoxide fumes in every gas fireplace, and get under every Christmas tree that is crooked to straighten it to a perfectly upright 90-degree angle.

Other reasons why Santa can't possibly be a man:

- Men can't pack a bag.
- Men would rather be dead than caught wearing red velvet.

- Men would feel their masculinity is threatened having to be seen with all those elves.

- Men don't answer their mail.

- Men aren't interested in stockings unless somebody's wearing them.

- Having to do the ho-ho-ho thing would seriously inhibit their ability to pick up women.

- Santa remembers it's Christmas. Enough said.

- Reads children's letters in office instead of in bathroom.

- Never explains what exactly you did to deserve that coal in your stocking; if you have to ask, maybe that's the problem!

- Despite the closet full of red coats with big black belts, still insists she has nothing to wear on Christmas Eve.

- "Mrs. Claus" wears work boots, has a crew cut and drives a 1968 El Camino.

- A man simply would not care if you were naughty or nice.

- Actually seems to shake like *two* bowls full of jelly.

- Bowl full of jelly, my ass. It's water retention.

- Constantly whining about equality until it's time to clean out the reindeer stalls.

- Matching shoes and belt? Only a woman would accessorize a pantsuit like that!

- No guy would ever name his animals Dancer and Prancer.

- Santa has never, ever been observed peeing off of rooftops.
- The most popular North Pole movie on Netflix is *The Notebook*.
- With the way they build chimneys these days you'd have to be a supermodel just to get in!
- Finally, being responsible for Christmas would require a commitment.

I can buy the fact that other mythical characters are men. Father Time shows up once a year unshaven and looking ominous. Definite guy. Cupid flies around carrying weapons. Uncle Sam is a politician who likes to point fingers. Any one of these individuals could pass the testosterone-screening test. But not St. Nick. Not a chance. However, as long as we have each other, good will, peace on earth, faith and Nat King Cole's version of "The Christmas Song," it probably makes little difference what gender Santa is. I just wish she'd quit dressing like a guy.

Santa Could Never Be a Woman: An Argument from a Man's Point of View

Some say Santa is a woman. I say no way! There is absolutely NO way Santa is female. Here's why.

First, Christmas would be late every year. The line at the department store would never move because Santa would feel the need to bond with every kid that sat on her lap. The elves would never get any toys made because they'd be too busy telling her, "No, Santa, those red pants do not make you look fat."

What woman would be caught dead in a chimney? Gosh, she might break a nail in there. Also, men don't care if they get covered with ashes and soot while sliding down the chimney.

Two prostitutes, after Christmas holidays:

"What did you ask Santa Claus to give you?"

"Hundred dollars, as usual."

If Santa was female, she sure wouldn't have white hair. And she would never wear a hat because it would mess up her hair. And what about the beard? I'm sure you'll agree that most women look significantly better without facial hair. Besides, she-Santa would not go out without makeup.

The tradition is for cookies and milk to be left for Santa on Christmas Eve. If Santa were a woman, the tradition would be chocolates and lattes. Also, a male Santa would judiciously take a bite from each cookie to prove he was there. If Santa was a woman, the whole darn box of Snackwells would be devoured and there'd be a sea of empty Ben & Jerry's containers all over the kitchen floor.

Santa doesn't need to ask directions; he instinctively knows where he's going. A female Santa would try to use landmarks, but up in the sky there are no landmarks and no place to ask directions. Besides, she-Santa would never go out driving in the snow and rain at night. She would make Mr. Claus do it and then complain about the way he drove.

Santa Claus: What's that terrible racket outside?

Mrs. Claus: It's rain, dear.

She-Santa would never say "HO HO HO." She would analyze it too much and think it was somehow demeaning.

Would any self-respecting female Santa really be seen wearing the same outfit year after year? No, she would have to have a new one each year. And red would not be the color. It would be more like pink or purple.

She-Santa would not clean up the mess that the deer make. Like you are going to make the deer wait until they get back to the North Pole? Men have years of training with dogs.

Yup, Santa's a guy all right!

The Claus Wedding Night

On her wedding night, a middle-aged Mrs. Claus turns to her new husband and says, "Please be gentle; I'm still a virgin."

"How the hell can you be a virgin?" asks Santa. "You've been married three times before you met me!"

"Well," says the new Mrs. Claus, "my first husband was a gynecologist, and all he wanted to do was look at it. My second husband was a psychiatrist, and all he wanted to do was analyze it. Then there was my third husband. He was an elf in the North Pole post office. He was responsible for licking stamps, and all he wanted to do was.... I do miss him sometimes!"

Top 10 Reasons Why a Woman WOULD LIKE to be Santa Claus

10. There'd be no more early morning decisions about what to wear to the office.

9. No one would bother to ask her for a ride to work.

8. Buy one big black belt and she'd be accessorized for life.

7. She would always work in sensible footwear.

6. She would never be expected to make the coffee.

5. There'd be no need to play office politics; a hearty ho-ho-ho would remind everyone who is the boss.

4. Juggling work and family would be easy. All her children would adore her; even her teenagers would want to sit in her lap.

3. She would never take the wrong coat on her way home.

2. She could grow a tummy the size of Texas and consider it a job requirement.

1. She could give all her ex-boyfriends lumps of coal for Christmas.

Santa on Trial

You are charged, Mr. Santa Claus, alias Saint Nick, alias Kris Kringle, age unknown, with the following offenses:

- failing to apply for landed immigrant status from Finland to the North Pole

- crossing the Canada–U.S. border illegally on December 24 of each year as far back as records go

- failing to operate a union toy shop, and not paying your elves the minimum wage, providing paid vacations or wages at time and a half for more than 40-hour work weeks
- failing to transmit employment insurance payments, income tax deductions and pension payments to the proper authorities on behalf of your employees
- failing to file a flight plan for your travels
- failing to equip your vehicle with seat belts or properly fitting your reindeer with emission control devices
- illegally administering an unauthorized drug to Rudolph to make his nose light up
- illegal entry of millions of homes on December 24 of each year
- not declaring as taxable income the cookies and milk left for you by millions each year
- and finally, parking in a no parking zone, namely rooftops, and having no record of either a driver's or pilot's license ever being issued in either Canada or the United States.

Faced with these charges and understanding their severity, have you any statement to make before I…wish you a Merry Christmas, a Happy New Year and dismiss all charges?

Santa walks into a bar…yet again…

After another tough Christmas Eve, Santa is in need of a drink so he walks into a bar and demands a shot of 12-year-old Scotch. The bartender thinks, "This guy doesn't know the difference," so he pours a shot of two-year-old Scotch.

Santa takes one sip and spits it out. He promptly hollers at the bartender, "I said 12-year-old Scotch, you bozo! I am Santa Claus. You can't fool me!"

Still unimpressed, the bartender pours some six-year-old Scotch. Santa takes a sip...same reaction. But the bartender still doesn't believe Santa knows the difference. So he pours a shot of 10-year-old Scotch. Again, same reaction from Santa. Finally, the bartender is convinced. He pours a glass of 12-year-old Scotch. Santa takes a sip and is most satisfied.

All the while this has been going on, a drunk at the end of the bar has been watching. He slides a shot glass down the bar to Santa and drunkenly says, "Hey mishter, tashte this!"

Santa obliges...and promptly spits it out. "It tastes like piss," Santa shoots back at the drunk.

The drunk replies, "It ish. How old am I?"

An Open Letter

Dear Friends,

I have been watching you very closely to see if you have been good this year, and you have. That's the good news. The bad news is that I was going to bring you all gifts from the "Twelve Days of Christmas," but we had a little problem. The 12 drummers drumming have all come down with VD from banging the eight maids a-milking, the 10 lords a-leaping have knocked up the nine ladies dancing, and the 11 pipers piping have been arrested for doing weird things with their pipes to the seven swans a-swimming, which, along with the six geese a-laying, four calling birds, three French hens, two turtle doves and the partridge, have me up to my sled runners in bird sh*t.

On top of all that, Mrs. Claus is going through menopause, my reindeer are in heat, the elves have joined the gay liberation movement, and some people who can't read a calendar have scheduled Christmas for the 5th of January. Maybe next year I will be able to get my act together and bring you the things you want. This year I suggest you get your asses down to Walmart before everything is gone.

Love,

Santa

Naughty Wife

Santa comes home from another long, hard Christmas Eve and finds Mrs. Claus having sex with some guy on the living room sofa.

"Mrs. Claus, what in the name of Rudolph's red nose are you doing?!" he asks.

Mrs. Claus looks at the guy and says, "See, I told you he was kinda dumb."

An Honest Letter to Santa

Dear Santa,

We're worried about you. From your rosy red cheeks to your legendary girth to your all-night sleigh ride around the world, you may be at risk for diseases, maladies, mishaps and lawsuits that send chills through our Santa-loving hearts.

Rosacea is a skin condition that affects millions of Americans, particularly at middle age. Although we're unable to examine you personally, based on a well-circulated report that your "cheeks were like roses, (your) nose like a cherry," we advise you to see a North Pole dermatologist.

Sadly, many observers conclude that your red skin condition comes from hitting the Christmas punch bowl a little too hard. Sadder still, rosacea can be aggravated by holiday stress, hot chocolate and overexertion—all things you may encounter this time of year. The one bright note is that certain antibiotics can help, but your facial tint is only our latest source of concern. A careful examination of what we know about you and your lifestyle raises a host of other trouble signs.

Obesity: Frankly, Santa, this should be your biggest area of concern. Studies show overweight men have more than double the normal risk of heart attacks and increased chances of many other diseases. We've seen the pictures; we've noticed you in the malls. And we've heard that your tummy shakes "like a bowlful of jelly" when you chuckle. For this, we'll take part of the blame. All these years, we've set out milk and cookies on Christmas Eve. With 102 million homes in the U.S. alone, even if 1 in 100 homes put out two cookies and a cup of milk, that would make an overnight snack of 2 million cookies and 63,750 gallons of milk. Maybe it's time for Mrs. Claus to get you a NordicTrack or a Thigh-master. But be sure to have the old ticker checked out before you start an exercise regimen.

Pipe smoking: You're often pictured with a pipe, and even though an apologist in the *New York Times* once claimed it's only a prop, one witness who encountered you in his home said, "the smoke it encircled his head like a wreath." According to the Fred Hutchinson Cancer Research Center, pipe and cigar smokers have twice a nonsmoker's risk for lung cancer, four times the risk for larynx cancer and two to three times the risk for cancers of the mouth and esophagus. Even if the pipe's just a prop, it might be a good idea to lose it. Remember, you're not just a saint, you're a role model.

Stress: Dealing with Christmas wishes from millions of kiddies could certainly put one on the emotional roller coaster. And anxiety can surpass even smoking as a risk factor for certain heart problems. On this point, though, we have some good news: a medical news service says laughter—as evidenced by your trademark "Ho, ho, ho"—is one of the best stress-busters.

Soot: We admire your ability to slide up and down the chimney, an average opening of about 12 inches by 16 inches. But creosote flakes on the chimney walls are toxic and can lead to respiratory problems.

Chimney sweeps never actually go into a chimney, and they wear protective masks when they reach up through the fireplace to vacuum the soot. We suggest you follow their lead and at the very least, wear a mask.

Repetitive strain injury (RSI): Cards and letters by the bagful arrive on your doorstep every year through regular mail, but this year we've noticed you're also receiving—and answering—e-mail. We applaud your move onto the information super-highway, with this caution: too much keyboard work can result in painful injuries to the hands, wrists and arms.

Deer mites: Close, continuous contact with your trusty reindeer means if they get mites, so might you. Take precautions.

So in conclusion, Santa, take care of yourself. The world needs you alive. We want to see a healthy Santa, with a six-pack instead of a beer belly. You're not getting any younger.

Sincerely,

The World

The Clauses

Saint Nicholas is the main Clause.

His brother is a relative Clause.

His children are dependent Clauses.

His Dutch uncle is a restrictive Clause.

Santa's elves are subordinate Clauses.

Santa's Complaint

Merry Christmas my ass. You think you got it bad? All night long, soot up my nose, stinkin' socks, double barrel buckshot up my butthole, drivin' all night in the f*ckin' snow. Hell, last year I damn near got sideswiped by a 747! And now Mrs. Claus is pissed off because she found panties in the sleigh and lipstick on my collar.

And that ain't all! Donner, Blitzen and Rudolph all got the shits over Albuquerque and now my sleigh is a mess! Those worthless f*cking elves won't clean it unless I pay them double time, the little bastards!

I'm so sick of milk and cookies, I could barf! Hell, the only highball I had all night was when I slipped getting out of the sleigh and racked myself. My bladder is so weak that I pissed my pants at 20,000 feet and froze to the f*cking seat.

Wait…there's more! All of a sudden I'm allergic to pine needles and holy sh*t, do my balls itch! Oh great! I think my hemorrhoids are back again.

Ho! Ho! Ho! Merry f*ckin' Christmas.

Santa Claus

Mall Santa

Because of my fluency in American Sign Language, I was hired to be a Santa Claus at the mall. My employer wanted to provide hearing-impaired children with a Santa who could communicate with them.

I sat for hours, performing for the children who came to visit. But none of them was deaf. Then, two girls approached shyly. One explained that her sister was deaf and could not speak.

"What is your name?" I signed slowly.

"J-A-S-M-I-N-E," she replied with her fingers, grinning from ear to ear.

I was bubbling over with pride when I absent-mindedly signed, "My name is H-E-N-R-Y, nice to meet you."

Top 10 Signs of Trouble in Santa Claus's Marriage

10. He's replaced some of the elves with scantily clad swimsuit models.

9. Mrs. Claus calls him "tubby piece of shit."

8. Instead of his reindeer and sleigh he gets around in a 1995 Camry.

7. He looks at Mrs. Claus and hums "Grandma got run over by a reindeer" whenever she walks into the room.

6. He spends hours behind closed doors with his very handsome elf friend Bruce.

5. Mrs. Claus spends all her time on Chaturbate.

4. He knows when she's been sleeping, he knows when she's awake, because he's wired the bedroom.

3. Mrs. Claus keeps flirting with the elves.

2. Stockings aren't the only things he's been nailing in front of the fireplace.

1. Creatures keep stirring in Santa's pants.

Department Store Santa Peeves

- Kids who refuse to believe that it's fruitcake on your breath and not gin.
- When the last guy to use the beard leaves bits of his lunch in it.
- Even while wearing the costume, people recognize you from *Crime Watch*.
- Parents who get all uptight when you offer their kids a swig from your hip flask.
- Enduring the taunts of your old buddies from Drama School.
- Those dorks in the Power Rangers costumes get all the babes.
- Kids who don't understand that Santa's been a little jittery since he got back from 'Nam.
- Two words: lap rash.

Santa in the Real World

To: All home managers, Mental Health Care Ltd.

From: Head nurse, General Hospital

Date: December 25

Re: S. Claus

We are having problems with the above-named. He presents as being happy and jolly and walks around saying "Ho ho ho." Additionally, he has taken to referring to an imaginary animal called Rudolph and insists on wearing a red and white coat and carrying a large sack. He refuses to use the front door, preferring to come down the chimney.

This behavior became problematic when he came down the dining room chimney because it has been bricked up for some time. When he is out in the community, he approaches young children of either sex and asks them to sit on his knee. Without staff intervention, he would then ask them if they want a present.

> **Q:** What does Father Christmas write on his Christmas cards?
>
> **A:** ABCDEFGHIJKMNOPQRSTUVWXYZ (No L!).

In short, his behavior makes his return to the community unlikely. I would be grateful for your advice concerning his suitability for a placement with Mental Health Care Ltd.

Thank you.

⚔ CHAPTER TWO ⚖

North Pole Humor

*Just in case you forgot, the names of Santa's reindeer are Dasher, Dancer, Prancer, Vixen, Comet, Cupid, Donner and Blitzen.

Air Traffic

Santa Claus, like all pilots, gets regular visits from the Federal Aviation Administration, and it was shortly before Christmas when the FAA examiner arrived.

In preparation, Santa had had the elves wash the sled and bathe all the reindeer. Santa had gotten his logbook out and made sure all his paperwork was in order.

The examiner walked slowly around the sled. He checked the reindeer harnesses, the landing gear (hooves) and Rudolph's nose. He painstakingly reviewed Santa's weight and balance calculations for sled's enormous payload.

Finally, he was ready for the inspection ride. Santa got in and fastened his seatbelt and shoulder harness and checked the compass. Then the examiner hopped in carrying, to Santa's surprise, a shotgun.

"What's that for?" asked Santa incredulously.

The examiner winked and said, "I'm not supposed to tell you this, but you're gonna lose an engine on takeoff."

Punishing Elves

Up north in Santa's village, an elf was caught stealing reindeer.

Santa was so mad that he undressed the elf and tied him to a birch tree. He was to stand there during the night as a suitable punishment.

The next morning Santa came to untie the elf. "I hope the mosquitos were really bad last night!" he said.

Reindeer sex toy:
a dil-doe.

"Oh, the mosquitos were nothing compared to that weaning reindeer calf that couldn't find its mother!" replied the elf.

King Rudolph

There was once a great king known as Rudolph the Red. One day he stood looking out the windows of is palace while his wife, Queen Katerina, sat nearby, knitting. He turned to her and said, "Look, my dear, it has begun to rain!"

Without even looking up from her knitting she replied, "It's too cold to rain. It must be sleeting."

The king shook his head and said, "I am the king of all the land, and Rudolph the Red knows rain, dear!"

Reindeer pick-up line:
"What do you say we go back to my place for some reindeer games?"

Revised Schedule for the North Pole Workers Union

Effective immediately, the following economizing measures are being implemented in the "Twelve Days of Christmas" subsidiary:

1. The partridge will be retained, but the pear tree, which never produced the cash crop forecasted, will be replaced by a plastic hanging plant, providing considerable savings in maintenance.

2. Two turtle doves represent a redundancy that is simply not cost effective. In addition, their romance during working hours could not be condoned. The positions are, therefore, eliminated.

3. The three French hens will remain intact. After all, everyone loves the French.

4. The four calling birds will be replaced by an automated voicemail system, with a call-waiting option. An analysis is underway to determine who the birds have been calling, how often and how long they talked.

Q: What do all the female reindeer do when Santa is busy working with the males on Christmas Eve?

A: Go into town and blow a couple bucks!

5. The five golden rings have been put on hold by the Board of Directors. Maintaining a portfolio based on one commodity could have negative implications for institutional investors. Diversification into other precious

metals, as well as a mix of bonds and stocks, appears to be in order.

6.   The six geese-a-laying constitute a luxury that can no longer be afforded. It has long been felt that the production rate of one egg per goose per day was an example of the general decline in productivity. Three geese will be let go, and an upgrading in the selection procedure by personnel will assure management that, from now on, every goose hired will be a good one.

7.   The seven swans-a-swimming is obviously a number chosen in better times. The function is primarily decorative. Mechanical swans are on order. The current swans will be retrained to learn some new strokes, thereby enhancing their outplacement.

8.   As you know, the eight maids-a-milking concept has been under heavy scrutiny by the ethics commission. A male/female balance in the workforce is being sought. The more militant maids consider this a dead-end job with no upward mobility. Automation of the process may permit the maids to try a-mending, a-mentoring or a-mulching.

9.   The nine ladies dancing have always been unnecessary. This function will be phased out as these individuals grow older and can no longer do the steps.

10. Ten lords-a-leaping is overkill. The high cost of lords, plus the expense of international

air travel, prompted the Compensation Committee to suggest replacing this group with ten out-of-work automobile industry workers. While leaping ability may be sacrificed, the savings are significant as we expect an oversupply of the unemployed this year.

11/12. Eleven pipers piping and 12 drummers drumming is a simple case of the band getting too big. A substitution with a string quartet, a cutback on new music and doing away with uniforms will produce savings that will drop right to the bottom line.

Overall, we can expect a substantial reduction in assorted people, animals and related expenses. Though incomplete, studies indicate that stretching deliveries over 12 days is inefficient. If we can ship in one day, service levels will be improved.

Regarding the lawsuit filed by the Attorneys' Association seeking expansion to include the legal profession ("thirteen lawyers suing"), a decision is pending.

Q: What's the difference between snowmen and snow-women?

A: Snowballs.

Day Off

One morning an elf phoned Santa. "I need a day off today; something is wrong with my eyes."

"What's wrong with your eyes?" asked Santa.

"I don't know, but I can't see myself coming into work today."

Directions

It is Christmas Eve and Santa is busy flying from house to house, guided by Rudolph and all the other magical reindeer. Next stop is Billy's house, so Santa screams his order to land. For some reason, the reindeer suddenly land on top of an outhouse. Santa looks around for a moment, then hollers, "No, Rudolph! I said the SCHMIDT house!"

Top 15 Reindeer Games

15. Strip poker with Mrs. Claus
14. Attach the Mistletoe to Santa's Ass
13. Spin the Salt Lick
12. Crapping down the chimneys of non-believers
11. Moose or Dare
10. Reindeer base jumping (no need for parachutes)
9. Bait-and-Shoot Elmo
8. The annual "Turn Frosty Yellow from 50 Paces" contest
7. Scare the Holy Crap Out of the Airline Pilot
6. Convince the Elves to Eat "Raisinets"
5. Pin the Tail on Rudolph's Ass
4. Hide the Venison Sausage with Vixen
3. Elf tossing
2. Sniff the Tail on the Donkey
1. The "Rudolph the Sh*t-faced Reindeer" drinking game

Rudolph the Red-nosed Wino

Rudolph the red-nosed wino,
Had a very shiny nose,
And if you got too near him,
He would take off all his clothes.

All of the other winos,
Used to laugh and call him names,
They never let poor Rudolph,
Join in any wino games.

Then one chilly Christmas Eve,
Rudolph froze to death in an alley.

   End of story.

Reindeer Reality

   According to the Alaska Department of Fish and Game, while both male and female reindeer grow antlers every summer (the only members of the deer family, Cervidae, to have females that do so), male reindeer drop their antlers at the beginning of winter, usually late November to mid-December. Female reindeer retain their antlers till after they give birth in spring. Therefore, according to every historical rendition depicting Santa's reindeer, every single one of them, from Rudolph to Blitzen, had to be a girl.

Did you hear about Adolph, the brown-nosed reindeer? He could run as fast as Rudolph, he just couldn't stop as fast.

A reindeer walks into a bar...

One evening, at a busy lounge in the deep south, a reindeer walked through the door, bellied up to the bar and ordered a martini. Without batting an eye, the bartender mixed and poured the drink, set it in front of the reindeer and accepted the twenty-dollar bill from the reindeer's hoof.

As he handed the reindeer some coins in change, he said, "You know, I think you're the first reindeer I've ever seen in here."

The reindeer looked hard at the hoofful of change and said, "Hmmmpf. Let me tell you something, buddy. At these prices, I'm the last reindeer you'll see in here."

New Job

A man walked into a kebab shop and was surprised to see Santa Claus serving behind the counter.

"Santa!" he said. "What are you doing working here? Shouldn't you be up at the North Pole preparing for the big day?"

Q: What do reindeer say before telling you a joke?

A: This one will sleigh you!

Santa let out a long sigh. He had really fallen on hard times. The red suit was splattered with chili sauce and bits of lettuce, his apron was a mess, and he looked as if the last thing in the world he wanted to be doing was serving kebabs. Eventually he admitted, "I'm afraid my business has gone belly up. What with the credit crunch and the recession, the toy industry took a hammering. I had to lay off some of the elves, the bank wouldn't give me a loan, and we just lost our competitive edge. Finally the receivers came in, asset-stripped the business and we went into liquidation."

"I'm really sorry to hear that," said the man. "It kind of makes us lose the tradition of Christmas along with you."

"I know," said Santa. "Anyway, enough of me and my troubles. What can I get you?"

The man said, "I'll have a large donair."

Q: Why is a reindeer like a gossip?

A: Because they are both tail bearers!

"Sorry," said Santa. "We are all out of Donner. Will Blitzen do instead?"

Pull Over

A cop on duty Christmas Eve pulls over Santa Claus. Getting out of his car, he walks over to the sleigh and says, "Do you know why I pulled you over?"

Santa replies, "No, officer, I don't."

"Well, I suspect that all of your reindeer are on drugs."

"Well, of course they are," says Santa.

Surprised, the officer asks, "Why are they on drugs?"

"How else do you think I get them flying high?"

North Pole News

REINDEER RESTRUCTURING

The recent announcement that Donner and Blitzen have elected to take the early reindeer retirement package has triggered a good deal of concern about whether they will be replaced, and about other restructuring decisions at the North Pole.

Streamlining was appropriate in view of the reality that the North Pole no longer dominates the season's gift distribution business. Home shopping channels and mail order catalogs have diminished Santa's market share, and he could not sit idly by and permit further erosion of the profit picture.

Rejected Christmas reality show: When Reindeer Attack!

The reindeer downsizing was made possible through the purchase of a late-model Japanese sled for the CEO's annual trip. Improved productivity from Dasher and Dancer, who summered at the Harvard Business School, is anticipated and should take up the slack with no discernible loss of service. Reduction in reindeer will also lessen airborne emissions, for which the North Pole has been cited and received unfavorable press.

Rudolph's role will not be disturbed. Tradition still counts for something at the North Pole. Management denies, in the strongest possible language, the earlier leak that Rudolph's nose got that way not from the cold, but from substance abuse. Calling Rudolph "a lush who was into the sauce and never did pull his share of the load" was an unfortunate

Q: Why does Scrooge love Rudolph the Red-nosed Reindeer?

A: Because every buck is dear to him.

comment, made by one of Santa's helpers and taken out of context at a time of year when he is known to be under executive stress.

Today's global challenges require the North Pole to continue to look for better, more competitive ways of doing business. It is not beyond consideration that deeper cuts may be necessary in the future to stay competitive. Forewarned is forearmed.

Breaking News

NORTH POLE (API)—Microsoft announced an agreement with Santa Claus Industries to acquire Christmas at a press conference held via satellite from Santa's summer estate somewhere in the southern hemisphere. In the deal, Microsoft will gain exclusive rights to Christmas, the reindeer, and other unspecified inventions. In addition, Microsoft will gain access to millions of households through the Santa Sleigh.

The announcement also included a notice that, beginning December 9, 2013, Christmas and the reindeer names will be copyrighted by Microsoft. This unprecedented move was facilitated by the recently acquired MS Court. Microsoft stated its commitment to "all who have made Christmas great" and vowed to "make licensing of the Christmas and reindeer names available to all." It is believed that the guidelines for licensing these names, due before Halloween, will be very strict.

When asked, "Why buy Christmas?" Bill Gates replied, "Microsoft has been working on a more efficient delivery mechanism for all of our products for some time, and recognized that the Santa Sleigh has some immediate benefits. We'll use it first for the next release of Windows and Office 2013."

In a multimedia extravaganza, the attendees were shown a seemingly endless video stream of products that make up the deal. It ended with a green and red version of the Microsoft logo and a new Christmas trademark, leading into the announcement of the first product from the deal.

Vixen, the new Director of Holidays and Celebrations said, "The first step is to assimilate Christmas within the Microsoft organization. This will take some time, so don't expect any changes this year." She continued, "Our big plans are for next year, when we release Christmas 2014. It will be bigger and better." She further elaborated that "For this year, Windows 8 users who sign up with MS Network will get sneak previews of Christmas 2013 as early as November 1."

Q: How do you make a slow reindeer fast?

A: Don't feed it!

Christmas 2013 is scheduled for release in December 2013, though one unnamed source said that it is dangerously close to the end of the year and may slip into the first half of 2014. An economist at Goldman Sachs explained that a slip would be catastrophic to next year's economy and the nation's tax revenue, possibly requiring the IRS to move the deadline for filing income tax returns to three months after Christmas, whenever that was. "But it could be good in the long term," he explained. "With Microsoft controlling Christmas, we may see it move to May or June, which are much slower months for retailers. With Thanksgiving remaining a late fall holiday, this may serve to even out the economy over the year."

Q: Where do you find reindeer?

A: It depends on where you leave them!

When asked if other holidays are being considered, Mr. Gates explained that "Christmas is the flagship of holidays, so we wanted to start there. Not all holidays are available for sale, and the remaining will have to show a good long-term business," suggesting that holidays with a short history may not be in the plans.

Though specific terms of the agreement were withheld, a Santa official confirmed that the deal was "sizeable, even for a man of Santa's stature." Some analysts think that Santa has saturated the holiday market and is looking for a means to expand his business to year-round products and services. Others contend that the jolly man is just looking to retire.

A spokesperson for the reindeer could not be reached for comment.

Facebook Status Update

Rudolph: My back is killing me. The sleigh would be a lot easier to pull if the driver didn't weigh almost 800 lbs.

Prancer, Mrs. Claus and Carl the Head Elf "like" this status.

Blitzen: He weighs only 800 lbs?!

Cupid: OMG LOL. Like totally funny dude.

Comet: We do all the work and he gets all the credit. Ho Ho Ho my ass.

Santa: Did you guys forget you friended me? You're all fired! And Mrs. Claus, I'll talk to you later.

Lost Reindeer

Santa gave an elf the job of looking for his lost reindeer. To help him, he hired an Inuit hunter. The two of them set off on their journey to find the reindeer. After riding awhile, the Inuit gets off his sled, puts his ear to the ground and says, "Hmmm, reindeer come."

Q: Why does Santa's sled get such good mileage?

A: Because it has long-distance runners on each side.

The elf scans the area with his binoculars, but sees nothing. He is confused and says to the Inuit guide, "I do not see anything, how do you know reindeer come?"

The Inuit replies, "Ear sticky."

Female Elf Employment Application

Form 69

1. Name: _____

2. Address: _____

3. Age: _____
(If under 100, parental permission is required)

4. Height: _____
(If over 3 feet 6 inches, please attach signed waiver)

5. Present Occupation: _____
(If politician, forget it!)

6. Hobbies: _____
(If boys, boys, boys, do you like "little, little" boys?)

7. Professional Qualifications: _____
(Can you cook, sew, clean and other things male chauvinist elves get off on?)

8. References: _____
(No religious references please. They tend to lead us astray.)

9. Have you ever been arrested or convicted for molesting a reindeer?
Yes ( ) No ( )
(If yes, you need not apply!)

10. Have you ever been arrested or convicted for molesting little elves?
Yes ( ) No ( )
(If yes, when can you start?)

11. Please list five personal references. All must be older than 10 and still believe in Santa Claus.
(Good Luck!)

Gifting

On Christmas morning, Rudolph is having a good moan to Prancer and Dancer. He says to them, "Santa has got me the wrong Christmas present—I'm beginning to think he might be dyslexic."

"What makes you think that?" they ask.

"Because he got me a Pony Sleigh Station."

Top 5 Elf Pet Peeves

5. Toil for 364 days a year just to make children smile, and no one gives a rip. Meanwhile, frolic around one day in some stupid outfit in February with a lousy bow and arrow and all of a sudden you're a hero.

4. Icy cold North Pole temperature makes it hard to produce quality workmanship.

3. Reindeer game #12: Elf Lacrosse.

2. Constantly ridiculed for that 0–854 record in the North Pole Basketball League.

1. Jolly ol' St. Nick has never yet brought back a single cookie to share.

CHAPTER THREE

Naughty and Nice

In the Christmas Mood

One night in December there was a romantic full moon, and Pedro said, "Hey, *mamacita*, let's do weeweechu."

"Oh no, not now, let's look at the moon!" said Rosita.

"Oh, c'mon baby, let's you and I do weeweechu. I love you and it's the perfect time," Pedro begged.

"But I just want to hold your hand and watch the moon," replied Rosita.

"Please, *corazoncito*, just once, do weeweechu with me."

Rosita looked at Pedro and said, "Okay, one time, we'll do weeweechu."

So Pedro grabbed his guitar and they both sang, "Weeweechu a merry Christmas, weeweechu a merry Christmas, weeweechu a merry Christmas, and a happy New Year."

Q: What do you get if you cross Raquel Welch and Santa Claus?

A: A thank-you card from Santa.

Top 10 Things Said at Christmas that Sound Dirty, but Aren't

10. Did you get any under the tree?
9. I think your balls are hanging too low.
8. Check out Rudolph's honker!
7. Santa's sack is really bulging.
6. Lift up the skirt so I can get a clean breath.
5. Did you get a piece of the fruitcake?
4. I love licking the end until it's really sharp and pointy.
3. From here you can't tell if they're artificial or real.
2. Can I interest you in some dark meat?
1. To get it to stand up straight, try propping it against the wall.

What a Girl Wants for Christmas

The Santa Claus at the shopping mall was very surprised when Emily, a young lady aged about 20 years old, walked up and sat on his lap. Now, we all know that Santa doesn't usually take requests from adults, but she smiled very nicely at him, so he asked her, "What do you want for Christmas?"

"Something for my mother, please," replied Emily sweetly.

"Something for your mother? Well, that's very loving and thoughtful of you," smiled Santa. "What would you like me to bring her?"

Emily answered smoothly, "A son-in-law."

Loving Gift

My husband gave me a mood ring for Christmas. When I'm in a good mood it turns green. When I'm in a bad mood, it leaves a red mark on his forehead.

A Poem

He laid her on the table,
So white, clean and bare.
His forehead wet with beads of sweat,
He rubbed her here and there.

He touched her neck and then her breast,
Then drooling felt her thigh.
The slit was wet and all was set,
He gave a joyous cry.

The hole was wide, he looked inside,
All was dark and murky.
He rubbed his hands and stretched his arms,
And then he stuffed the turkey.

All She Wants for Christmas

It's December, and a married woman goes to see her doctor and tells him that all she wants for Christmas is for her husband to be interested in sex. The doctor then proceeds to give her a bottle of pills. He tells her to give them a try and then let him know how it's working.

So she takes the pills home and a few days later puts one in her husband's Christmas dinner. That night, they make love for one hour. The next day, she's running around thrilled and happy. *I can't believe how well that worked*, she thinks to herself. That night she puts two pills in his food and they make love for two hours. The next day, she's even hornier, so she dumps all the pills in his food.

Three weeks have gone by without any word from this woman, so the doctor decides to give her a call. A little boy answers the phone. The doctor says, "Little boy, is your mother home?"

"No, she's... Who's this?" the little boy asks.

"I'm a friend of your mother's, and I gave her some pills to help her out a few weeks ago. Maybe you know how it's going."

"That was you?!" the little boy says. "Let me tell you: Mom's dead, my sister's pregnant, my ass hurts, and Dad's in the attic going, 'Here kitty, kitty, kitty.'"

Barbie's Dream Man

A little girl is in line to see Santa. When it's her turn, she climbs up on Santa's lap. Santa asks, "What would you like Santa to bring you for Christmas?"

The little girl replies, "I want a Barbie and G.I. Joe."

Santa looks at the little girl for a moment and says, "I thought Barbie came with Ken."

"No," says the little girl. "She comes with G.I. Joe. She fakes it with Ken."

'Twas the Night for Some Nooky

'Twas the night before Christmas,
And the house was all neat.
The kids were both gone,
And my wife was in heat.

The doors were all bolted,
And the phone off the hook,
It was time for some nooky,
By hook or by crook.

Mama in her teddy,
And I in the nude,
Had just hit the bedroom
And reached for the lube.

When out on the lawn
There arose such a cry,
That I then lost my boner
And mama went dry.

Up to the window
I sprang like an elf,
Tore back the shade
While she played with herself.

The moon on the crest
Of the snowman we'd built,
Showed a broom up his ass,
Clean up to the hilt.

When what to my wondering
Eyes should appear,
But a rusty old sleigh
And eight mangy reindeer.

With a fat little driver,
Half out of his sled,
A sock in his ear,
And a bra on his head,

Sure as I'm speaking,
He was as high as a kite,
And he yelled to his team,
But it didn't sound right:

"Whoa Sh*thead, whoa A**hole,
Whoa Stupid, whoa Putz,
Either slow down this rig
Or I'll cut off your nuts.

"Look out for the lamp post,
And don't hit the tree,
Quit shaking the sleigh,
'cause I gotta go pee."

They cleared the old lamp post,
The tree got a rub,
Just as Santa leaned out,
And threw up on my shrub.

And then from the roof,
We heard such a clatter,
As each little reindeer
Now emptied his bladder.

I was donning my jacket
To cover my ass,
When down our poor chimney
Santa came with a crash.

His suit was all smelly
With perfume galore,
He looked like a bum,
And smelled like a whore.

"That was some brothel,"
He said with a smile,
"The reindeer are pooped,
I'll just stay here awhile."

He walked to the kitchen,
Poured himself a drink,
Then whipped out his pecker
And p*ssed in the sink.

I started to laugh,
My wife smiled with glee,
The old boy was hung
Nearly down to his knee.

Back in the den,
Santa reached in his sack,
But his toys were all gone,
And some new things were packed.

The first thing he found
Was a pair of false tits,
The next was a handgun
With a shaft that spits.

A box filled with condoms
Was Santa's next find,
And a six-pack of panties,
The edible kind.

A bra without nipples,
A penis extension,
And several other things
That I shouldn't even mention.

A garter, a G-string,
And all types of oil,
And a dildo so long
That it lay in a coil.

"This stuff ain't for kids,
Mrs. Santa will sh*t,
So I'll leave it right here,
And now I'll just split."

He filled every stocking
And then took his leave,
With one tiny butt plug
Tucked under his sleeve.

He sprang to his sleigh,
But his feet were like lead,
Thus he fell on his ass
And broke wind instead.

In time he was seated,
Took the reigns of his hitch,
Said, "Take me home, Rudolph,
The night's been a b*tch!"

The sleigh was near gone
When we heard Santa shout,
"The best thing about p*ssy
Is that you can't wear it out!"

Top 10 Reasons a Christmas Tree is Better than a Man

10. A Christmas tree doesn't mind getting dressed up.

9. A Christmas tree is always erect.

8. Even a small one gives satisfaction.

7. A Christmas tree stays up for 12 days and nights.

6. A Christmas tree always looks good—even with the lights on.

5. A Christmas tree is always happy with its size.

4. A Christmas tree has cute balls.

3. A Christmas tree doesn't get mad if you break one of its balls.

2. You can throw a Christmas tree out when it's past its "sell by" date.

1. You don't have to put up with a Christmas tree all year.

Mistletoe

Jennifer was a pretty 18-year-old girl. In the week before Christmas she sauntered up to the craft counter and was trying to decide which of the many types of tinsel she would buy. Finally, she made her choice and asked the spotty youth who was manning the section, "How much is this gold tinsel garland?"

The spotty youth pointed to the Christmas mistletoe above the counter and said, "This week we have a special offer: just one kiss per yard."

"Wow, that's great," said Jennifer. "I'll take 12 yards."

With expectation and anticipation written all over his face, the boy measured out the garland, wrapped it up and gave it to Jennifer.

She then called to an old man who had been browsing through the Christmas trees and said, "My grandpa will settle the bill."

Yo mama so fat, I took a Polaroid of her last Christmas, and it's still printing.

Tattoos

A woman goes into a tattoo parlor and tells the tattoo artist that she wants a tattoo of a turkey on her right thigh, just below her bikini line. She also wants him to put the words "Happy Thanksgiving" under the turkey.

So the guy does it, and it comes out looking really good. The woman then instructs him to put a Santa Claus with "Merry Christmas" on her left thigh just below the bikini line. So the guy does that one, and it turns out pretty good as well.

As the woman is getting dressed to leave, the tattoo artist says, "If you don't mind, could you tell me why you had me put such unusual tattoos on your thighs?"

She replies, "I'm sick and tired of my husband complaining all the time that there is nothing good to eat between Thanksgiving and Christmas!"

Things Said about Christmas Dinner that Sound Dirty, but Aren't

- Wow, that's one terrific spread.
- I'm in the mood for a little dark meat.
- Tying the legs together keeps the inside moist.
- That's a big breast.
- If I don't undo my pants, I'll burst.
- Please come again.
- It's a little dry; do you still want to eat it?
- Don't play with your meat!
- I didn't expect everybody to come at once.
- You got a little bit on your chin.
- How long will to take after you stick it in?
- How long do I have to beat it?
- That's the biggest one I've seen!
- It must be broken because when I squeeze the tip, nothing squirts out.

Sexual Torture Christmas

'Twas the night before Christmas,
And all through the house,
The Masters were spanking
Their Frauleins and Fraus,

Mistress and switch
In black leather and chains,
Were chastising their subbies
With paddles and canes,

When down in the dungeon
There came such a clatter,
I jumped from my chair
To see what was the matter.

Jumped up, tripped over,
And fell on my face—
Forgot that my domme
Had just lashed me in place!

Away to the window
I made a mad dash,
Threw open the window,
Felt the cool air on my ass.

And then through the smoke
And the snow and the swirls,
Came a rusty old sleigh
Drawn by twelve pony girls.

With bells on their nipples
And stripes on their asses,
They pulled and they strained,
Those twelve little lasses.

The drunken old driver
Stood holding his d*ck;
I knew by the "red nose"
That this was old Nick.

Slower than snails,
His chargers they came,
And he whipped and he flailed
As he called them by name:

"Come Karen and Janet
And Anna and Tammy,
Pull the sleigh on
Or I'll paddle your fanny.

And Connie and Jo
And Britney and Jilly,
With your blazing red asses
You look somewhat silly.

Susan and Tina
And Billie and Kay,
You bend yourselves over;
It's floggings today."

Up on the roof he went,
Stumbled and fell,
And down the chimney he came,
Screaming like hell.

He staggered and stumbled
Over to the door,
Tripped over a flogger
We'd left on the floor.

I heard him exclaim
As he drove out of sight,
"Merry Christmas you kinksters,
And to all a good night!"

Good Vibrations

A few days after Christmas, an old lady goes into a sex shop and says to the clerk, "G-g-good mo-mo-morning! Ca-can you h-h-h-he-elp me?"

"I'll try," says the clerk. "What can I do for you?"

"D-d-do you s-s-sell vi-vi-vibrators?" asks the woman.

"Yes we do," says the clerk.

"I-ieee g-got th-this M-Ma-Ma-Magic Thruster f-fo-for Christmas. Do you ca-ca-carry it?" she asks.

"Yes, we have that one in stock," says the clerk. "It comes in small, medium and large, and in a variety of colors."

"D-d-does it vvv-v-vibrate on d-d-different speeds?"

"Yes," says the clerk. "You can set it for slow speed, medium or orgasmic."

"Th-th-th-that's the one!" says the woman.

"Great. Would you like me to wrap one up for you?"

"Nnn-n-n-no," says the woman. "Th-th-th-th-that wo-wo-won't be necessary. I ju-ju-just have one qu-qu-question ab-abba-about it. H-how d-d-d-do you t-t-t-turn it OFF!"

CHAPTER FOUR

Presents!

The Mailman's Present

A mailman is trudging through the snow carrying a huge sack of mail at Christmas time. As he is stuffing a stack of envelopes in one mailbox on his route, the door of the house opens and a beautiful woman beckons him to come inside out of the cold.

After serving the mailman a warm drink, the woman invites him to stay for lunch. After a sumptuous meal, she disappears into her bedroom and returns wearing only skimpy lingerie. She proceeds to lure the mailman into her bed, where they spend the rest of the afternoon.

As he prepares to leave, the mailman says, "You know, I've delivered the mail for almost 20 years, and I've never experienced anything like this before. Why did you decide to do all this for me?"

"Well, actually," the woman replies, "it was my husband's idea."

"Your husband's idea?" says the mailman incredulously.

"Yeah," replies the woman. "I was writing out our Christmas shopping list, and when I asked him what we should get for the mailman, he said, 'Aw, f*ck him.' But the lunch was my idea."

Gifts from Chuck

On the eighth pain of Christmas,
Chuck Norris sent to me:
Eight tears a-sulking,
Seven teeth a-spitting,
Six punches a-hitting,
Five painful swings,
Four dying herds,
Three dead men,
Two knuckle shoves,
And destruction with only one knee.

Something Really Cheap

About a week before Christmas, Tom thought he'd better buy his wife a gift.

"How about some perfume?" he asked the cosmetics clerk. She showed him a bottle costing $50.

"That's a bit much," said Tom, so she pulled out a smaller bottle for $30.

"That's still quite a bit," Tom groused.

Growing disgusted, the clerk brought out a tiny $15 bottle.

Tom grew agitated. "What I mean," he said, "is I'd like to see something really cheap."

So the clerk handed him a mirror.

Q: What was so good about the neurotic doll the girl was given for Christmas?

A: It was wound up already.

Crappy Gift

A boy opens his Christmas present to find nothing but an empty shoe box. His parents told him it was an Action Man Deserter.

Top 10 Things to Say About Gifts You Don't Like

10. Boy, if I hadn't recently shot up four sizes, that would've fit.
9. It would be a shame if the garbage man ever accidentally took this from me.
8. It's perfect for wearing in the basement!
7. Well, well, well...
6. I really don't deserve this.
5. Gosh, I hope this never catches fire!
4. I love it, but I fear the jealousy it will inspire.
3. If the dog buries it, I'll be furious!
2. Sadly, tomorrow I enter the federal witness protection program.
1. To think I got this the year I vowed to give all my gifts to charity.

Forgetful Husband

Bob was in trouble. He forgot to buy his wife a Christmas present. His wife was really p*ssed. She told him, "Tomorrow morning, I expect to find a gift in the driveway that goes from 0 to 200 in less than six seconds, AND IT BETTER BE THERE!!"

The next morning he got up early and left for work. When his wife woke up, she looked out the window, and sure enough there was a box gift-wrapped in the middle of the driveway—clearly not the sports car she had specifically asked for. Curious, she put on her robe, ran out to the driveway and brought the box back into the house. In the box was a brand-new bathroom scale.

Bob has been missing since Friday.

An Amazing Gift

One Christmas Eve, a frenzied young man ran into a pet shop looking for an unusual Christmas gift for his wife. The shop owner suggested a parrot named Chet who could sing famous Christmas carols. This seemed like the perfect gift.

"How do I get him to sing?" the young man asked excitedly.

"Simply hold a lighted match directly under his feet," was the shop owner's reply.

The shop owner held a lighted match under the parrot's left foot. Chet began to sing: "Jingle bells! Jingle bells!…" The shop owner then held another match under the parrot's right foot. Chet's tune changed: " Silent night, holy night…"

The young man was so impressed that he paid the shop owner and ran home as quickly as he could with Chet under his arm. When his wife saw her gift, she was overwhelmed.

"How beautiful!" she exclaimed. "Can he talk?"

"No," the young man replied, "But he can sing. Let me show you."

So the young man whipped out his lighter and placed it under Chet's left foot, as the shop owner had shown him, and Chet crooned: "Jingle bells! Jingle bells!..." The man then moved the lighter to Chet's right foot, and out came: "Silent night, holy night..."

The wife, her face filled with wonder, then asked, "What if we hold the lighter between his legs?"

The man did not know. "Let's try it," he answered, eager to please his wife.

Q: What did the bald man say when he got a comb for Christmas?

A: Thanks. I'll never part with it.

So they held the lighter between Chet's legs. Chet twisted his face, cleared his throat, and then the little parrot sang out loudly like it was the performance of his life: "Chet's nuts roasting on an open fire..."

A Christmas Engagement

A man walks into a jewelry store to buy his girlfriend an engagement ring that he plans on giving her for Christmas. Looking behind the glass case, he comes across an exquisite band with a handsome-sized rock in its center.

"Excuse me, sir," the gentleman says to the salesman. "How much is this ring?"

"Ah, that's a beautiful piece," the salesman replies. "It goes for $10,000."

"Holy crap!" the man exclaimed. "That's a lot of money!"

"Yes, but a diamond is forever."

"Perhaps," the gentleman replied, "but my marriage won't last that long!"

The Perfect Fit

A young man wishes to buy his girlfriend a Christmas gift. As they have not been dating very long, he decides that a pair of gloves will strike just the right note—romantic, but not too personal.

Unfortunately, the clerk assigned to wrapping the Christmas gifts is wrapping a pair of silk panties for someone else and mistakenly mixes up the packages. When the young man's girlfriend opens her gift and find the panties, she reads this note:

"Darling,

I chose these because I noticed that you are not in the habit of wearing any when we go out in the evening. I thought about buying you the long ones with buttons but decided on the short ones because they are so easy to remove. I bought you white ones because the lady I bought them from showed me a pair she had been wearing for three weeks and they were hardly soiled. I had her try yours on and she looked really smart. I even tried to get them on but they were too small for me. But if you like them I might get a different pair for me.

I wish I could be there to put them on you for the first time, as no doubt other hands will come into contact with them before I have the pleasure of seeing you in them. When you take them off, please remember to blow in them before putting them away as they will naturally be a little damp from wearing. I can hardly wait to see you in them. Please be sure to wear them for our upcoming date."

Special Christmas

John is trying to find out what his wife, Mary, wants for Christmas. "Would you like a new mink coat?" he asks.

"Not really," says Mary.

"Well how about a new Mercedes sports car?" says John.

"No, thank you," she responds.

"What about a new vacation home by a lake?" he suggests.

She again rejects his offer.

Frustrated, he finally asks, "Well what would you like for Christmas?"

"John, I'd like a divorce," answers Mary.

John thinks for a moment and replies, "Sorry, dear, I wasn't planning to spend that much."

The Ultimate Gift

Just before the start of Christmas vacation, the teacher asks the members of the class what gifts they hope to receive for the holidays.

"A set of electric trains," says Jimmy.

"A new iPod," says Mary.

"A box of Tampax," adds Benny.

"Tampax?" exclaims the teacher. "What on earth are you going to do with Tampax?"

"Anything I want. I keep hearing on TV how with Tampax you can go biking, camping, swimming, horseback riding…"

A Letter to Santa from Barbie

Dear Santa:

Listen, you ugly little troll, I've been helping you out every year, playing at being the perfect Christmas present, wearing skimpy bathing suits in frigid weather and drowning in fake tea from one too many tea parties, and I hate to break it to you, but it is DEFINITELY payback time. There had better be some changes around here this Christmas, or I'm going to call for a nationwide meltdown—and trust me, you won't want to be around to smell it. So, here's my holiday wish list.

1. A nice, comfy pair of sweat pants and a frumpy, oversized sweatshirt. I'm sick of looking like a hooker. How much smaller are these bathing suits going to get? Do you

have any idea what it feels like to have nylon and velcro crawling up your butt?

2. Real underwear that can be pulled on and off. Preferably white. What bonehead at Mattel decided to cheap out and *mold* imitation underwear to my skin?! It looks like cellulite!

3. A real man...maybe G.I. Joe. Heck, I'd take Tickle-Me Elmo over that wimped-out excuse for a boytoy Ken—seriously, what's with that earring anyway? And if I'm going to have to suffer with him, at least make him (and me) anatomically correct.

4. Arms that actually bend so I can push the aforementioned Ken-wimp away once he is anatomically correct.

5. A new career. Pet doctor and school teacher just don't cut it. How about a systems analyst? Better yet, a public relations senior account executive!

6. A new, millennium-appropriate persona. Maybe "PMS Barbie," complete with a miniature container of chocolate chip cookie dough ice cream and a bag of chips; or "Animal Rights Barbie," outfitted with a fake fur coat, my very own paint gun, a bottle of spray-on blood and handcuffs; or "Stop Smoking Barbie," sporting a removable nicotine patch and equipped with several packs of gum.

7. No more McDonald's endorsements. The grease is wrecking my vinyl.

8. Mattel stock options. It's been decades; I think I deserve it.

Okay, Santa, that's it. Considering my valuable contribution to society, I don't think these requests are out of line. If you disagree, then you can find yourself a new Barbie for next Christmas. It's that simple.

Yours truly,

Barbie

Ken's Letter to Santa

Dear Santa,

I understand that one of my colleagues has petitioned you for changes in her contract, specifically asking for anatomical and career changes. In addition, it is my understanding that disparaging remarks were made about me, my ability to please and some of my fashion choices. I would like to take this opportunity to inform you of some of my issues concerning Ms. Barbie, and some of my own needs and desires.

First of all, I along with several other colleagues, feel Barbie does NOT deserve any more preferential treatment—the b*tch has everything. Neither I, nor G.I. Joe, Jem, Raggedy Ann and Andy, have a dream house, a Corvette, evening gowns or, in some cases, the ability to change our hairstyle. I personally have only three outfits that I am forced to mix and match at great length. But the decision to accessorize my outfits with an earring was mine and reflects my lifestyle choice.

I, too, would like a career change. Have you ever considered "Decorator Ken," "Beauty Salon Ken" or "Out of Work Actor Ken"? In addition, there are several other avenues that could be considered such as "S&M Ken," "Green Lantern Ken," "Circuit Ken," "Bear Ken" or "Master Ken." These would more accurately reflect my desires and perhaps open up new markets.

And as for Barbie needing bendable arms so she can push me away, I need bendable knees so I can kick that b*tch to the curb. Bendable knees would also be helpful for me in other situations—we've talked about this issue before.

In closing, I would like to point out that any further concessions to the blonde bimbo from hell will result in action being taken by myself and others. And Barbie can forget about having G.I. Joe; he's mine—at least that's what he said last night!

Sincerely,

Ken

Santa's Replies to Barbie and Ken

Dear Barbie,

You must have been blind. All the elves knew Ken batted for the other team. Even Rudolph and the rest of the reindeer knew.

As for your demands, we will not be meeting any of them, as you are no longer beloved by little girls.

Today's modern little girl does not want to grow up striving to be the prettiest girl with an eating disorder. You and your fake hair, nails, breasts, lips—heck, all of you, can go to hell! Girls want positive role models, not a doll that is dumb enough to fall in love with the gayest man to ever live. So you can take your anatomically incorrect body and join the other reject toys in the historical garbage bin.

F*ck you.

Santa

P.S. That night we spent together meant nothing.

> **Q:** What do you give a train driver for Christmas?
> **A:** Platform shoes.

Dear Ken,

Call me.

Santa

Christmas Request

Dear Santa,

All I ask for this year is a big, fat bank account and a slim body. Please don't mix these up like you did last year.

Thanks,

Ungrateful

What to Do with an Ugly Sweater

A promising New Year has begun! Your annoying Aunt Matilda has gone home. Now what should you do with that gruesome sweater she so generously gave you for Christmas? Here are some creative ideas.

1. Regift the ugly thing to your worst enemy.
2. Wash it repeatedly in hot water. Convert the ghastly thing into a snug outfit for your chihuahua.
3. Wrap the awful, unsightly thing around a two-by-four. Makes a great scratch post for your kitty.
4. Dip that sweater in soapy water. Use it to dislodge grime from your car's hubcaps.
5. Add it to the compost pile.
6. Cut it into small squares to glue under the legs of wobbly furniture.
7. Make a hideous (but practical) seat cover for your child's Big Wheel.
8. With a little imagination, convert the horrid sweater into a colorful welcome mat. (Good for wiping feet.)
9. Convert it into thermal underwear. After all, thermal underwear is supposed to be itchy.
10. Wear the darn thing.

Thank-you Notes

One Christmas, a mother decreed that she was no longer going to remind her children of their thank-you note duties. As a result, their grandmother never received acknowledgments of the generous checks she had given.

The next year things were different, however.

"The children came over in person to thank me," the grandparent told a friend triumphantly.

"How wonderful!" the friend exclaimed. "What do you think caused the change in behavior?"

"Oh, that's easy," the grandmother replied. "This year I didn't sign the checks."

Twelve Days of Christmas Thank-you Letters

December 25

Dearest Dave,

I went to the door today, and the postman delivered a partridge in a pear tree. This was a delightful gift! I couldn't have been more surprised or pleased, darling!

With truly the deepest love,

Agnes

December 26

Dearest Dave,

Today the postman brought me yet another of your sweet gifts. The two turtle doves that arrived today are adorable, and I'm delighted by your thoughtful and generous ways.

With all of my love,

Agnes

December 27

Dearest Dave,

You've truly been too kind! I must protest; I don't deserve such generosity. The three French hens amaze me! Yet, I am not surprised—what more should I expect from such a nice person?

Love,

Agnes

December 28

Dear Dave,

Four calling birds arrived at my door today. They are truly nice to listen to, but don't you think that enough is enough? You are being too romantic.

Affectionately,

Agnes

December 29

Dearest darling Dave,

It was a lovely surprise to get five golden rings! I now have one for every finger. You truly are impossible, darling, yet oh how I love it! Quite frankly, all of those squawking birds from the previous days were starting to get on my nerves. Yet, you managed to come through with a beautiful gift!

All my love,

Agnes

December 30

Dear Dave,

When I opened my door this morning, there were actually six geese a-laying on my front steps. So you're back to the birds again, huh? Those geese are dear, but where will I keep them? The neighbors are complaining, and I am unable to sleep with all the racket. Please stop, dear.

Cordially,

Agnes

December 31

Dave,

What is with you and these stupid birds?! Seven swans a-swimming! What kind of sick joke is this? There are bird droppings everywhere! They never shut up, and I don't get any sleep! I'm a nervous wreck! It's not funny, you weirdo, so stop with the birds.

Sincerely,

Agnes

January 1

Okay, wise guy, the birds were bad enough. Now what do you expect me to do with eight maids a-milking? And their cows?! The front lawn is now completely ruined by them, and I can't move in my own house! Just lay off me, or you'll be sorry!

Agnes

January 2

Hey loser,

What are you? You must be some kind of sadist! There are now nine ladies dancing! There is only one problem with that! They're dancing 24 hours a day, which is upsetting the cows and the maids. The cows can't sleep, and they are sh*tting everywhere! The neighbors are getting up a petition to evict me, and I'm going out of my mind! You'll get yours!

Agnes

January 3

You rotten scum! What's with the ten lords a-leaping?! They are leaping across the rooms breaking everything and even injuring some of the maids and ladies! The place smells, is an absolute mad house, and is about to be condemned! At least the birds are quiet; they were trampled to death by the cows. I hope you are satisfied, you rotten, vicious, worthless piece of garbage!

From,

One who means it!

Q: Why did the girl change her mind about buying her grandmother a packet of handkerchiefs for Christmas?

A: She could not work out what size her nose was.

January 4

Listen, you evil, sadistic maniac! Now there are eleven pipers piping, and they certainly do play! They haven't stopped chasing those maids since they got here! Plus they're louder than those screeching birds ever were! The building commissioner has subpoenaed me to give cause as to why the house shouldn't be condemned! I can't even think of a reason! You creep! I'm calling the police!

Your sworn enemy,

Agnes

January 5

From: the Law Offices of Badger, Rees and Yorker

20 Knave Street

Chicago, Illinois

Dear Sir,

This is to acknowledge your latest gift of twelve drummers drumming, which you have seen fit to inflict on our client, one Agnes McHolstein. The destruction, of course, was total. If you attempt to reach Ms. McHolstein at Happy Daze Sanatorium, the attendants have instructions to shoot you on site. Please direct all future correspondence to this office. With this letter, please find attached service of a lawsuit filed on behalf of Ms. McHolstein.

Sincerely,

M. Rees, Esq.

Twelve Days After Christmas

The first day after Christmas,
My true love and I had a fight;
And so I chopped the pear tree down
And burnt it, just for spite.

Then with a single cartridge,
I shot the blasted partridge
That my true love, my true love,
My true love gave to me.

The second day after Christmas,
I pulled on old rubber gloves
And very gently wrung the necks
Of both the turtle doves.

The third day after Christmas,
My mother caught the croup;
I had to use the three French hens
To make some chicken soup.

The four calling birds were a big mistake,
For their language was obscene.
The five golden rings were completely fake
And turned my fingers green.

The sixth day after Christmas,
The six laying geese wouldn't lay,
So I sent the whole darn gaggle
To the A.S.P.C.A.

On the seventh day, what a mess I found;
The seven swans a-swimming had all drowned.
Swimmers they were not, those swans
My true love gave to me.

The eighth day after Christmas,
Before they could suspect,
I bundled up the rest of the gifts
And sent them back collect.

I wrote my true love, "We are through, love!"
And I said in so many words,
"Furthermore your gifts were for the birds!"

The 10 Worst Gifts to Buy a Woman (A Woman's Advice)

1. Never give a woman any kind of household appliance or something that is going to make housework "easier." For instance, a blender, toaster, vacuum, one of those mops they advertise on TV that does everything but suck the life out of you, anything in an infomercial. One allowable choice is a new washing machine with a turbo spin cycle. (Makes laundry day go by pretty fast when you can at least sit on it during spin-dry and end up smiling the rest of the day.)

2. Any bulk cleaning supplies: "Honey, I got you that large box of Tide you've been wanting." "This Windex should last you awhile." "I got a good deal on the industrial strength toilet

bowl cleaner." All I can say is, be prepared to run. I have faith that if you would have at least stopped and thought about it, you would have had the sense to spring for the $5 Chia Pet you were eyeing in K-mart.

3. Any sharp object made by Ronco that slices or dices, or a set of Ginsu knives. These may one day be used as a weapon against you when you come home with lipstick on your collar after a "night out with the boys."

4. Do not buy gifts for yourself and pretend they are for her: "Honey, I'm sure you'll get a lot of use out of the new drill I bought you." By then she will have put it to good use by drilling a quarter-inch hole into the side of your skull for even thinking she would like such a lame gift. After a gift like this, you probably won't be around for next Christmas.

5. Any lingerie made of flannel, such as a pair of feet pajamas with a trap door in back, or a Little Mermaid or Barney character night-gown. It gives her the idea that you do not consider her the beautiful woman that she is. Take out that wallet and buy her something sexy from Victoria's Secret (just like you did for your mistress or other girlfriend).

6. No-name perfume that costs you $1.99, such as Eau de Toilet, which actually smells like the bathroom, moldy fruit or your dirty socks. If you are going to buy her perfume, spring for the brand names.

7. Any type of cubic zirconia jewelry you see on the Home Shopping Network. It will be quite embarrassing when she is showing off that fabulous "diamond" to her friends and tries to cut glass with it (we actually do test them, you know). Also on the jewelry subject, now would not be a good time to buy her that set of diamond nipple clamps you always wanted to; you know how we like to show off our jewelry, and it could get embarrassing at the New Year's party when she decides to show them off to your buddies.

8. Please do not buy her clothes because you think for one minute you have good taste in women's clothing. Well, perhaps you might if you are a transvestite, but all in all, believe me, she'll smile and say it's beautiful while choking back tears and mumbling under her breath, "Where the hell would I ever wear this outfit without being arrested for bad taste?" An additional hint: plaids do not go with stripes (I know you think your golfing outfit looks just fine—it doesn't).

9. Do not give her a gift certificate to Jenny Craig or Weight Watchers. Most men know better, especially the ones who have learned the correct response to the "do these pants make me look fat" question. If you are one of the poor souls who still doesn't get it and you purchase a gift that in any way suggests she should lose weight, be prepared for the silent treatment for a month (although that may be

something you would actually look forward to). A better alternative would be hiring a Chippendale dancer as a personal trainer to get her motivated into getting fit.

10. Last but not least, never buy a woman anti-wrinkle cream, or a book on "how not to be nasty Sunday through Saturday." These are not considered gifts; they are considered reasons for seriously injuring the person who bought them and just may stand up in a court of law.

Nightgown

Looking in the mall for a cotton nightgown for myself, I tried my luck in a store known for its hot lingerie. To my delight, however, I found just what I was looking for.

Waiting in the line to pay, I noticed a young woman behind me holding the same nightgown. This confirmed what I suspected all along: despite being over 50, I still have a very "with it" attitude.

"I see we have the same taste," I said proudly to the 20-something behind me.

"Yes," she replied. "I'm getting this for my grandmother for Christmas."

Oops!

Last Christmas, Grandpa was feeling his age and found that shopping for Christmas gifts had become too difficult. So this year he decided to send checks to everyone instead. In each card he wrote, "Buy your own present!" and mailed them early.

He enjoyed the usual flurry of family festivities, and it was only after the holidays that he noticed he had received very few cards in return. Puzzled over this, he went into his study, intending to write a couple of his relatives and ask what had happened. It was then, as he cleared off his cluttered desk, that he got his answer. Under a stack of papers, he was horrified to find the gift checks that he had forgotten to enclose with the cards.

CHAPTER FIVE

F*cking Kids

At Grandma's

Two young boys were spending the night with their grandparents. Christmas was just a couple of weeks away, and at bedtime, when the two boys knelt beside their beds to say their prayers, the youngest one began praying at the top of his lungs: "I PRAY FOR A NEW BICYCLE, I PRAY FOR A NEW XBOX, I PRAY FOR A NEW PVR…"

His older brother leaned over and nudged him and said, "Why are you shouting your prayers? God isn't deaf."

To which the little brother replied, "No, but Grandma is!"

Blessing

A four-year-old boy was asked to give thanks before Christmas dinner. The family members bowed their heads in expectation. He began his prayer, thanking God for all his friends, naming them one by one. Then he thanked God for mommy, daddy, brother, sister, grandma, grandpa and all his aunts and uncles.

Then he began to thank God for the food. He gave thanks for the turkey, the stuffing, the fruit salad, the cranberry sauce, the pies, the cakes, even the whipped cream. Then he paused, and everyone waited...and waited. After a long silence, the young fellow looked up at his mother and asked, "If I thank God for the broccoli, won't he know that I'm lying?"

Train Schedule

A few days after Christmas, a mother working in the kitchen was listening to her son play with his new electric train set in the living room. She heard the train stop and her son said, "All you sons of b*tches who are getting off, get the hell off now, and all of you sons of b*tches who are getting on, get your asses on the train because we're leaving right now."

> Q: What's the most popular Christmas wine?
>
> A: I don't like Brussels sprouts!

The mother went into the living room and told her son, "We don't use that kind of language in this house. Now I want you to go to your room for two hours. When you come out you may play with your train, but you must use nicer language."

Two hours later, her son came out of his room and resumed playing with his train. Soon the train stopped, and the mother heard her son say, "All passengers who are disembarking the train, please remember to take all of your belongings with you. We thank you for riding with us today and hope that you will ride with us again. For those of you just boarding, we ask that you stow all hand luggage under your seat. Remember that there is no smoking except in the club car. We hope that you will have a pleasant and relaxing journey with us today. For those of you who are p*ssed off because of the two-hour delay, please see the b*tch in the kitchen."

A Letter from a Boy on the Naughty List

Dear Santa,

I've been good all year long. Okay, most of the time. Okay, there was this one time... Oh f*ck it, I'll buy my own sh*t!

Little Johnny

Santa Police

On Christmas morning, a cop on horseback is sitting at a traffic light, and next to him is a kid on his brand-new bike. The cop says to the kid, "Nice bike you got there. Did Santa bring that to you?"

The kid says, "Yeah."

The cop says, "Well, next year tell Santa to put a taillight on that bike." The cop then proceeds to issue the kid a $20.00 bicycle safety violation ticket.

The kid takes the ticket, and before the cop rides off, says, "By the way, that's a nice horse you got there. Did Santa bring that to you?"

Humoring the kid, the cop says, "Yeah, he sure did."

The kid says, "Well, next year, tell Santa to put the d*ck underneath the horse, instead of on top."

Bad Leroy

Little Leroy went to his mother demanding a new bicycle. His mother decided that he should take a look at himself and the way he acts. She said, "Well, Leroy, Santa didn't bring you one for Christmas, and we don't have the money to just go out and buy you anything you want. So why don't you write a letter to Jesus and pray for one instead."

After his temper tantrum, his mother sent him to his room. He finally sat down to write a letter to Jesus:

Dear Jesus,

I've been a good boy and would appreciate a new bicycle.

Your friend,

Leroy

Now, Leroy knew that Jesus really knew what kind of boy he was (a brat), so he ripped up the letter and decided to give it another try:

Dear Jesus,

I've tried to be a good boy, and I want a new bicycle.

Yours truly,

Leroy

Well, Leroy knew this wasn't totally honest, so he tore it up and tried again:

Dear Jesus,

I've thought about being a good boy, and can I have a bicycle?

Leroy

Well, Leroy looked deep down in his heart (which by the way was what his mother really wanted). He knew he had been terrible and was deserving of almost nothing. He crumpled up the letter, threw it in the trash can and went outside. He aimlessly wandered about, depressed because of the way he treated his parents, and really considered his actions. He finally found himself in front of a Catholic church. Leroy went inside and knelt down, not knowing what he should really do. Leroy finally got up and began to walk back toward the door, looking at all the statues. All of a sudden he grabbed a small one and ran out the door. He went home, hid it under his bed and wrote this letter:

Jesus,

I've got your mama. If you ever want to see her again, give me a bike!

Sincerely,

You know who

F*cking Presents

A little kid sits on Santa's lap, and Santa says, "What would you like for Christmas?"

The kid says, "A f*cking swingset for the backyard."

Santa says, "You'll have to ask nicer than that if you want Santa to bring you presents. Let's try again. What else would you like?"

The kid says, "A f*cking sandbox for the side yard."

Santa says, "That's no way to talk to Santa. One more time. What else would you like for Christmas?"

The boy thinks for a minute, and then he says, "I want a f*cking trampoline in the front yard."

Santa lifts the boy off his lap and goes to talk to the kid's parents. He tells them what the kid said to him, and then says to the parents, "I know how to stop it. Don't get him anything for Christmas except dog doo. Put a pile of dog doo in the backyard where he wants the swingset, put another pile in the side yard where he wants the sandbox, and another pile in the front yard where he wants the trampoline. That should make him change his tune."

Christmas morning, the kid goes downstairs to open his presents, but there aren't any. He runs out the back door, looks around, and comes back in. He runs out the side door, looks around, and comes back in. He runs out the front door, looks around, and comes back in, shaking his head.

His father says, "What's wrong, son?"

The kid says, "Santa brought me a f*cking dog, but I can't find him."

Done Being Good

Dear Santa,

You must be surprised that I'm writing to you today, the 26th of December. Well, I would very much like to clear up certain things that have occurred since the beginning of the month, when, filled with illusion, I wrote you my letter asking for a bicycle, an electric train set, a pair of roller blades and a football uniform.

I wore myself out studying until, not only was I the first in my class, but I also had the best grades in the whole school. There was no one in my entire neighborhood that behaved better than me, with my parents, my brothers, my friends and my neighbors. I would go on errands, and even help the elderly cross the street. There was virtually nothing within reach that I would not do for humanity.

So what balls do you have leaving me a f*cking yo-yo, a stupid whistle and a pair of socks?! What the f*ck were you thinking, you fat son-of-a-b*tch, that you've taken me for a sucker the whole f*cking year to come out with some sh*t like this under the tree?! As if you hadn't f*cked with me enough, you gave that little piece of sh*t across the street so many toys that he can't even walk into his house!

Please don't let me see you trying to fit your big fat ass down my chimney next year. I'll f*ck you up. I'll throw rocks at those stupid reindeer and scare them away so you'll have to walk back to the f*cking North Pole, just like what I have to do now since you didn't get me that f*cking bike. F*CK YOU, SANTA! Next year you'll find out how bad I can be, you fat bastard.

Sincerely,

Johnny

Optimism and Pessimism

A father had two little sons, one of whom was an eternal optimist, while the other was a perpetual pessimist. One Christmas he decided try to temper both of their proclivities: in addition to their standard gifts, he told them they'd each get something chosen especially for them. His plan was to give the pessimist every toy and game he could possibly desire, while the optimist would be directed to the basement filled with manure.

On Christmas, after the normal presents were opened, the father sent the optimist to the cellar and led the pessimist to the room filled with presents.

After the pessimist opened all the gifts, he turned to his father with a sad face and said, "What good is all this stuff? The TV will wear out, the XBOX will get smashed, and all the other toys will be broken within the week!"

After a few minutes of listening to such woe, the father remembered his optimistic son and ran to the basement steps.

There in the basement was his other son, swimming through the manure with a gleeful smile. The father asked him why he was so happy, to which the boy exclaimed, "With this much manure, there must be a pony in here somewhere!"

Joy Ride

It was the day after Christmas, and at a church in San Francisco, Pastor Mike was looking at the nativity scene outside when he noticed the baby Jesus was missing from the figures. Immediately, Pastor Mike turned toward the church to call the police. But as he was about to go inside, he saw little Jimmy with a red wagon, and in the wagon was the figure of the little infant Jesus.

Pastor Mike walked up to Jimmy and said, "Well, Jimmy, where did you get that little Jesus?"

Jimmy replied, "I got him from the church."

"And why did you take him?"

With a sheepish smile, Jimmy said, "Well, about a week before Christmas, I prayed to little Lord Jesus. I told him if he would bring me a red wagon for Christmas, I would give him a ride around the block in it."

Brothers!

On Christmas morning, two children are opening their presents. The younger boy gets a toy plane, a remote control tank, a BB gun, a new bike and an XBOX 360. The older boy gets a sweater and a book. The younger brother begins to taunt the older brother, saying "Look, I got way more presents than you."

The older brother replies, "Oh yeah? Well at least I don't have cancer!"

Bad Santa Answers Kids' Letters

Dear Santa
I wud like a kool toy space ranjur for Xmas. Iv ben a good boy all yeer.
YeR FReND,
BiLLy

Dear Billy,

Nice spelling. You're on your way to being a career lawn-care specialist. How about I send you a book so you can learn to read and write? I'm giving your older brother the space ranger—at least he can spell!

Santa

Dear Santa,

I have been a good girl all year, and the only thing I ask for is peace and joy in the world for everybody!

Love,
Sarah

Dear Sarah,

Your parents smoked pot when they had you, didn't they?

Santa

Dear Santa,

I've written you for three years now asking for a fire truck. Please, I really, really want a fire truck this year!

Love,
Joey

Dear Joey,

Let me make it up to you. While you sleep, I'm gonna torch your house. You'll have more fire trucks than you'll know what to do with.

Santa

Dear Santa,

I don't know if you can do this, but for Christmas, I'd like for my mommy and daddy to get back together. Please see what you can do.

Love,

Teddy

Dear Teddy,

What, and ruin that hot affair your dad's still having with the babysitter? He's banging her like a screen door in a hurricane, son! Let me get you some nice Legos instead.

Santa

Dear Santa,

I need more Pokemon cards, please! All my friends have more Pokemon cards than me. Please see what you can do.

Love,

Michelle

Dear Michelle,

It blows my mind. Kids are forcing their parents to buy hundreds of dollars worth of these stupid cards, and none of you snot-nosed brats are even learning to play the game. Let me get you something more your speed, like Chutes and Ladders.

Santa

Dear Santa,

I want a new bike, a PlayStation, a train, some G.I. Joes, a dog, a drum kit, a pony and a tuba.

Love,

Francis

Dear Francis,

Who names their kid "Francis" nowadays?

Santa

Dear Santa,

I left milk and cookies for you under the tree, and I left carrots for your reindeer outside the backdoor.

Love,

Susan

Dear Susan,

Milk gives me the sh*ts and carrots make the deer fart in my face. You want to be a kiss-ass? Leave me a glass of Chivas Regal and some Toblerone.

Santa

Dear Santa,

What do you do the other 364 days of the year? Are you making toys?

Your friend,

Thomas

Dear Thomas,

All toys get made in China. I have a condo in Vegas, where I spend most of my time squeezing cocktail waitresses' asses and losing all my cash at the craps table. Hey, you wanted to know.

Santa

Dear Santa,

Do you see us when we're sleeping, and do you really know when we're awake, like in the song?

Love,

Jessica

Dear Jessica,

You are that gullible? Good luck in whatever you do; I'm skipping your house.

Santa

Dear Santa,

I really, really want a puppy this year. Please, please, *please* could I have one?

Timmy

Dear Timmy,

That whiney begging sh*t may work with your folks, but that crap doesn't work up here. You're getting a sweater again.

Santa

Dearest Santa,

We don't have a chimney in our house; how will you get in to leave me my presents?

Love,

Marky

Dear Mark,

First, stop calling yourself "Marky"—that's why you're getting your ass whipped at school. Second, you don't live in a house, that's a low-rent apartment complex you're living in. Third, I get inside your pad just like all the burglars do: through your bedroom window. Sweet dreams!

Santa

Lost in the Mall

A little boy was lost at a large shopping mall during a busy Christmas season. He approached a uniformed security officer and said, "I've lost my dad!"

The security officer asked, "What's he like?"

The little boy replied, "Beer and women with big boobs."

You'd Better Be Good

Two-year-old Sarah and her five-year-old sister had been fighting a lot this year. Sarah's parents, trying to take advantage of their daughter's new-found interest in Santa Claus, reminded her that Santa was watching and doesn't like it when children fight. This warning had little impact.

"I'll just have to tell Santa about your misbehavior," the mother said as she picked up the phone and dialed. Sarah's eyes grew big as her mother asked "Mrs. Claus" (really Sarah's aunt; Santa's line was busy) if she could put Santa on the line. Sarah's mouth dropped open as her mom described to "Santa" (Sarah's uncle) how the two-year-old was acting. But, when her mom said that Santa wanted to talk to her, she reluctantly took the phone.

"Santa," in a deepened voice, explained to Sarah how there would be no presents Christmas morning for children who fought with their sisters. He would be watching, and he expected things to be better from now on.

Sarah, now even more wide-eyed, solemnly nodded to each of Santa's remarks and silently hung the phone up when he was done. After a long moment, her mother (holding in her chuckles at being so clever) asked, "What did Santa say to you, dear?"

In almost a whisper, Sarah sadly but matter-of-factly stated, "Santa said he won't be bringing toys to my sister this year."

Do You See What I See?

A father says to his son, "Did you see Father Christmas this year?"

"No," replies the boy, "it was too dark to see him. But I heard the nasty words he said when he stubbed his toe on the edge of my bed."

Christmas Play

When a kindergarten student playing Joseph in the school nativity play forgot his lines, a teacher prompted him from the side. She whispered, "You have traveled a very long way, Joseph. You are hot and tired. What do you think you would say to the innkeeper?"

The boy brightened up, wiped his brow and said with pride, "Boy, do I need a drink!"

Q: Did you hear about the Beverly Hills school Christmas pageant?

A: Two kids dressed as Mary and Joseph and they are on their way to the inn in Bethlehem. On the other side of the stage, a boy in a shepherd's outfit is on a cell phone, calling for reservations.

Do it Again!

A father asked his young daughter what she would like for Christmas. She said that what she wanted more than anything else was a baby brother. And it so happened that on Christmas Eve, her mother came from the hospital clutching a baby boy.

The following year, the father again asked his daughter what she would like for Christmas.

"Well," she replied, "if it's not too uncomfortable for Mommy, I'd like a pony."

Spelling

A little boy sits on Santa's lap. Santa says, "I bet I know what you want for Christmas," and with his finger he taps the boy's nose with every letter as he spells T-O-Y-S.

The little boy thinks a second and says, "No, I have enough toys."

Santa replies with another guess, once again tapping the boy's nose with every letter of C-A-N-D-Y.

Again the little boy thinks a second and says, "No, I have all kinds of candy."

"Well what would you like for Christmas?" Santa asks.

The little boy replies, tapping Santa on the nose, "P-U-S-S-Y, and don't tell me you don't have any because I can smell it on your finger!"

Chapter Six

Do You Believe?

Raising Funds

A preacher wanted to raise money for his annual Christmas drive for the poor, and being told there was a fortune to be made in horseracing around that time of year, he decided to purchase one and enter it in races. At the local auction, however, the going price for a horse was so steep that he ended up buying a donkey instead. The preacher decided that he might as well go ahead and enter the donkey in the races. He figured that because a donkey always features prominently in the manger scenes of Jesus' birth, his would be a festive addition to the races. To his surprise, the donkey came in third. The next day the racing sheets carried this headline:

PREACHER'S ASS SHOWS

The preacher was so pleased with the donkey that he entered it in another race, and this time it won. The headlines blared:

PREACHER'S ASS OUT IN FRONT

The bishop was so upset with this kind of publicity that he ordered the preacher not to enter the donkey in another race. The newspaper headline read:

BISHOP SCRATCHES PREACHER'S ASS

This was just too much for the bishop, and he ordered the preacher to get rid of the animal.

The preacher decided to give it to a children's orphanage as an early Christmas gift. The next day the headline announced:

CHILDREN HAVE THE BEST ASS IN TOWN

The bishop fainted when he saw it. He informed the children that they would have to dispose of the donkey, and they finally did to a farmer for ten dollars. The next day the paper announced the transaction:

BISHOP FORCES CHILDREN TO PEDDLE ASS FOR TEN BUCKS

The bishop died of a heart attack. Merry Christmas.

In Honor

Three men died on Christmas Eve and were met by Saint Peter at the Pearly Gates.

"In honor of this holy season," Saint Peter said, "you must each present something that symbolizes Christmas to get into heaven."

The first man fumbled through his pockets and pulled out a lighter. He flicked it on and said, "This represents a candle."

"You may pass through the Pearly Gates," Saint Peter said.

The second man reached into his pocket and pulled out a set of keys. He shook them and said, "They're bells."

Saint Peter let him pass through the Pearly Gates.

The third man was searching desperately through his pockets and finally pulled out a pair of women's panties.

St. Peter looked at the man with a raised eyebrow and asked, "And just what do those symbolize?"

The man replied, "They're Carol's."

Is There a Santa Claus? A Physicist's View

Consider the following:

1. Flying reindeer: No known species of reindeer can fly. But there are 300,000 species of living organisms yet to be classified, and while most of these are insects and germs, this does not completely rule out flying reindeer that only Santa has ever seen.

2. Number of households: There are 2 billion children (persons under 18) in the world. But because Santa doesn't (appear) to handle the Muslim, Hindu, Jewish and Buddhist children, that reduces the workload to 15 percent of the total: 378 million, according to the Population Reference Bureau. At an average (census) rate of 3.5 children per household, that's 91.8 million homes. One presumes there's at least one good child in each.

3. Time per visit: Santa has 31 hours of Christmas to work with, thanks to the different time zones and the rotation of the earth, assuming he travels east to west (which seems logical). Divided by the number of houses he must visit,

the math works out to 822.6 visits per second. This is to say that for each Christian household with good children, Santa has 1/1000th of a second to park, hop out of the sleigh, jump down the chimney, fill the stockings, distribute the remaining presents under the tree, eat whatever snacks have been left, get back up the chimney, back into the sleigh and move on to the next house.

4. Velocity: Assuming that each of these 91.8 million stops are evenly distributed around the world (which, of course, we know to be false but for the purposes of our calculations we will accept), we are now talking about .78 miles per household, a total trip of 75.5 million miles.

    This means that Santa's sleigh is moving at 650 miles per second—3000 times the speed of sound. For purposes of comparison, the fastest man-made vehicle on earth, the Ulysses space probe, moves at a poky 27.4 miles per second. A conventional reindeer can run, tops, 15 miles per hour.

5. Mass: The payload on the sleigh adds another interesting element. Assuming that each child gets nothing more than a medium-sized Lego set (2 pounds), the sleigh is carrying 321,300 tons, not counting Santa, who is invariably described as overweight.

    On land, conventional reindeer can pull no more than 300 pounds. Even granting that "flying reindeer" (see point #1) could pull 10 times that amount, eight, or even nine of them, cannot do the job. We need 214,200 reindeer. This increases the payload—not even counting the weight of the sleigh—to 353,430 tons.

6. Force: A mass of over 350,000 tons traveling at 650 miles per second creates enormous air resistance, which will heat the reindeer up in the same fashion as spacecraft re-entering the earth's atmosphere. The lead pair of reindeer will absorb 14.3 quintillion joules of energy. Per second. Each.

In short, they will burst into flame almost instantaneously, exposing the reindeer behind them, and create deafening sonic booms in their wake. The entire reindeer team will be vaporized within 4.26 thousandths of a second.

Santa, meanwhile, will be subjected to centrifugal forces 17,500 times greater than gravity. A 250-pound Santa (which seems ludicrously slim) would be pinned to the back of his sleigh by 4,315,015 pounds of force.

Q: A smart blonde, a blonde and Santa Claus jump off a bridge at the same time; which one hits the ground first?

A: The blonde—the other two don't exist.

In conclusion, if Santa ever did deliver presents on Christmas Eve, he's dead now.

Fish Seller

A boy is standing on a corner selling fish, calling to passersby, "Dam fish for sale, dam fish for sale."

A preacher walks by, hears the questionable language and asks, "Why are you calling them 'damn fish'?"

The kid says, "I caught them at the dam, so they're dam fish."

Realizing his mistake, and seeing as it is Christmas Eve, the preacher decides to buy some fish. He takes them home and says to his wife, "Cook the dam fish, please."

His wife looks at him with surprise and says, "Preachers aren't supposed to talk like that."

The preacher explains why they are called dam fish, and she agrees to cook them.

When dinner is ready and everyone is sitting down, the preacher asks his son to pass him the dam fish. His son replies, "That's the spirit, Dad! Pass the f*cking potatoes!"

Q: Who did the dyslexic Satanist worship?

A: Santa.

Little Johnny and the Devil

A Sunday school teacher asked little Johnny, "Do you believe in the Devil?"

"No," said Johnny. "It's the same as Santa Claus. I know it's my daddy."

Christmas Wishes

Cinderella was 75 years old. After a fulfilled life with the now dead prince, she contentedly sat in her rocking chair, watching the world go by from her front porch, with a cat called Alan for companionship. Then on Christmas day, out of nowhere appeared her Fairy Godmother. Cinderella said, "Fairy Godmother, what are you doing here after all these years?"

The Fairy Godmother replied, "Well Cinderella, it's Christmas, and since you have lived a good, wholesome life since we last met, I have decided to grant you three wishes. Is there anything for which your heart still yearns?"

Cinderella is taken aback, but after some thoughtful consideration and almost under her breath, she uttered her first wish: "I wish I was wealthy beyond comprehension."

Instantly, her rocking chair was turned into solid gold. Cinderella was stunned. Alan, her old faithful cat, jumped off her lap and scampered to the edge of the porch, quivering with fear. Cinderella said, "Oh thank you, Fairy Godmother!"

The Fairy Godmother replied, "It is the least I can do. What does your heart want for your second wish?"

Cinderella looked down at her frail body and said, "I wish I was young and beautiful again."

At once her wish, having been desired, became reality, and her beautiful, youthful visage had returned. Cinderella felt stirrings inside her that had been dormant for years, and long-forgotten vigor and vitality began to course through her very soul.

Then the Fairy Godmother again spoke: "You have one more wish; what shall you have?"

Cinderella looked over to the frightened cat in the corner and said, "I wish you to transform Alan, my old cat, into a beautiful and handsome young man."

Knock knock.
Who's there?
Mary.
Mary who?
Merry Christmas!

Magically, Alan suddenly underwent so fundamental a change in his biological make-up that, when complete, he stood before her the handsomest man she had ever seen, so fair indeed that birds began to fall from the sky at his feet.

The Fairy Godmother again spoke. "Congratulations and a Merry Christmas to you, Cinderella," she said. "Enjoy your new life." And, with a blazing shock of bright blue electricity, she was gone.

For a few eerie moments, Alan and Cinderella looked into each other's eyes. Cinderella sat, breathless, gazing at the most stunningly perfect young man she had ever seen. Then Alan walked over to Cinderella, who sat transfixed in her rocking chair, and held her close in his muscular arms. He leaned in close to her ear and, blowing her golden hair with his warm breath, whispered, "I bet you regret having my balls chopped off now, don't you?"

Swear Jar?

A man goes to church Christmas morning, and afterward, stops to shake the preacher's hand. He says, "Preacher, I'll tell you, that was a damned fine sermon. Damned good."

The preacher responds, "Thank you sir, but I'd rather you didn't use profanity in God's house."

The man continues, "I was so damned impressed with that sermon, I put five thousand dollars in the offering plate!"

The preacher doesn't hesitate replying, "No SH*T?!"

Three Wise Firemen

In a small southern town, I came across a nativity scene that showed great skill and talent had gone into creating it. One small feature confused me: the three wise men were wearing firemen's helmets.

Totally unable to come up with a reason or explanation, I continued on my way. At a Quik Stop on the edge of town, I asked the lady behind the counter about the helmets.

She exploded into a rage, yelling at me, "You stupid Yankees never do read the Bible!"

I assured her that I did, but simply couldn't recall anything about firemen in the Bible.

She jerked her Bible from behind the counter and ruffled through some pages, and finally jabbed her finger at a passage. Sticking it in my face she said, "See, it says right here: 'The three wise man came from afar.'"

Religious Glossary for Christmas Mass

Amen: the only part of a prayer that everyone knows.

Bulletin: your receipt for attending Christmas Mass.

Pew: a medieval torture device still found in Catholic churches.

Holy water: a liquid whose chemical formula is H_2OLY.

Incense: Holy smoke!

Hymn: a song of praise usually sung in a key three octaves higher than the congregation's range.

Choir: a group of people whose singing allows the rest of the congregation to lip-sync.

Ushers: the only people in the parish who don't know the seating capacity of a pew.

Relics: people who have been going to Mass for so long, they actually know when to sit, kneel and stand.

Kyrie eleison: the only Greek words that most Catholics can recognize besides "gyros" and "baklava." Also a hit pop song in the 1980s.

Processional: the ceremonial formation at the beginning of Mass consisting of altar servers, the celebrant and late parishioners looking for seats.

Recessional: the ceremonial formation at the conclusion of Mass led by parishioners trying to beat the crowd to the parking lot.

Magi: the most famous trio ever to attend a baby shower.

Manger: where Mary gave birth to Jesus because Joseph didn't have medicare coverage.

Saint Nicklaus: it turns out the real Santa Claus is not a jolly fat man in a red suit, but a pious Greek man who became the patron saint of pawnbrokers, thieves, archers, sailors and, lastly, children.

Virgin: what Mary was supposed to be. But c'mon, what is more likely: God impregnating her, or that she was a Jewish minx who lied to her fiancé about who the father was?

Once Upon a Perfect Night

Once upon a time, a perfect man and a perfect woman met. After a perfect courtship, they had a perfect wedding. Their life together was, of course, perfect.

One snowy, stormy Christmas Eve, this perfect couple was driving their perfect car (a Dodge Grand Caravan) along a winding road when they noticed someone at the side of the road in distress. Being the perfect couple, they stopped to help. There stood Santa Claus with a huge bag of toys. Not wanting to disappoint any children on Christmas, the perfect couple loaded Santa and his toys into their vehicle. Soon they were driving along, delivering the toys.

Unfortunately, the driving conditions deteriorated and the perfect couple and Santa Claus were in an accident. Only one of them survived.

Question: Who was the survivor?

Answer: The perfect woman. She's the only one who really existed in the first place. Everyone knows there is no Santa Claus, and there is no such thing as a perfect man.*

*Women, stop reading here. Men, keep going.

So, if there is no perfect man and no Santa Claus, the perfect woman must have been driving. This explains why there was a car accident.

Q: What did one angel say to the other?

A: Halo there!

They Grow Up So Fast

A man figured that his son, now at the age of seven, would inevitably begin to have doubts about Santa Claus. Sure enough, one day the boy announces, "Dad, I know something about Santa Claus, the Easter Bunny and the Tooth Fairy."

"Okay, son," says the father, taking a deep breath. "Let's hear it. What do you know?"

The boy replies, "They are all nocturnal."

Service

Jack was filing out of church on Christmas Eve, and the pastor was standing at the door as he always does to shake hands. The pastor grabbed Jack by the hand, pulled him aside and said to him, "You need to join the Army of the Lord!"

Jack replied, "I'm already in the Army of the Lord, Pastor."

The pastor questioned, "How come I don't see you except at Christmas and Easter?"

Jack took a quick look around and whispered back, "I'm in the Secret Service."

Monastery

At a monastery high in the mountains, the monks have a rigid vow of silence. Only at Christmas can they speak, and then only two words, and only to the head monk.

On his first Christmas there, Brother Thomas is allowed to speak and he says, "More blankets."

Silence ensues for 364 days.

The next Christmas, Brother Thomas says to the head monk, "More food."

Once again, silence for 364 days.

The following Christmas, when Brother Thomas speaks to the head monk he says, "I'm leaving."

The head monk responds, "Good. You've done nothing but b*tch since you got here."

Minister

The minister of a church enjoyed a drink now and then, but his passion was for peach brandy. One of his congregants was a friend who would make him a bottle each Christmas.

One year, when the minister went to visit his friend, hoping for his usual Christmas present, he was not disappointed, but his friend told him that he had to thank him for the peach brandy from the pulpit the next Sunday.

In his haste to get the bottle, the minister hurriedly agreed and left. It wasn't until the next Sunday that he suddenly remembered that he had to make a public announcement that he was being supplied alcohol from a member of the church. That morning, his friend sat in the pew with a grin on his face, waiting to see the minister's embarrassment.

The minister climbed into the pulpit and said, "Before we begin, I have an announcement. I would very much like to thank my friend, Joe, for his kind gift of peaches...and for the spirit in which they were given!"

Heavenly Christmas Sermon

Father O'Toole was about to deliver his sermon at Midnight Mass on Christmas Eve, and the church was absolutely full to overflowing with lovely people full of Christmas cheer. But before he got started, he wanted to clear something up. Father O'Toole, the priest of a small Irish village, kept a rooster and 10 hens in the hen house behind the church, but when he went to feed the birds earlier that day, he discovered that the cock was missing. He knew about cock fights happening in the village— "entertainment" over the long winter—so he decided to question his parishioners in church that evening. He asked, "Has anybody got a cock?"

All the men stood up.

"No, no," he said, "that wasn't what I meant. Has anybody seen a cock?"

All the women stood up.

"No, no," he said, "that wasn't what I meant. Has anybody seen a cock that doesn't belong to them?"

Half the women stood up.

"No, no," he said, "that wasn't what I meant. Has anybody seen MY cock?"

Sixteen altar boys, two priests and a goat stood up.

The priest fainted.

The Hippie and the Nun

A hippie with long hair and a beard got on a bus, headed back home for the holidays. The bus was very crowded, and the man took a seat next to a young nun. She was very beautiful, and he was surprisingly attracted to her. After getting his courage up, he finally said to the nun, "Will you have sex with me?"

The nun, disgusted, told the bus driver to stop the bus and she got off. The man was very disappointed, and he moved up to the front of the bus to wait for his stop. Seeing that the young hippie was upset, the bus driver decided to help him out. He said to the young man, "I know that nun. Every night, she goes to the graveyard at nine o'clock to pray at the statue of Jesus. Being it's Christmas time, there is no way she would turn down God's request. Just go there tonight and tell her that you are Jesus and ask her to have sex with you."

This gave the hippie great hope. He decided to put off going home for a few hours and went to the grave-yard that night. Sure enough, there was the nun. As she kneeled down, he decided to make his move. Dressed in a white robe with a hood, he walked over to the nun and said, "I am Jesus Christ. I have come back for this holiday season and I have one request. Will you have sex with me?"

Now, of course the nun could not deny the power of God and his almighty son, so she agreed. "I just have one request," said the nun. "It has to be anal sex so I can remain a virgin and continue in my sisterhood."

The disguised hippie agreed, and the two had sex. When they were done, the man thought that it would be funny to reveal his identity to the nun. He took off his robe, revealing his tie-dyed shirt, ripped jeans and hemp necklace. "Hahaha. I'm not Jesus. I'm the hippie from the bus!" he exclaimed.

Much to the young man's surprise, the nun took off her habit, revealing a gray shirt and gray pants. Laughing, he yelled, "Hahaha. I'm not the nun. I'm the bus driver!"

Chuck and Jesus

Long ago, Chuck Norris didn't care about remembering when Jesus' birthday was, so he just so happened to send him a birthday card on December 25. Jesus was too scared to correct Chuck Norris, and to this day, Christmas is celebrated on December 25.

Damn Christmas

A woman is out Christmas shopping with her three young children. After hours of trailing around toy shops and hearing her kids asking for every item on the shelves, she is thoroughly fed up. Weighed down with bags, she squeezes herself and her kids into a crowded shopping mall elevator, sighs loudly and mutters, "Whoever started this whole Christmas thing should be arrested and strung up!"

A voice from the back of the elevator replies, "Don't worry, ma'am; I believe they crucified him."

The Virgin Birth

A woman takes her 16-year-old daughter to the doctor. The doctor says, "Okay, Mrs. Jones, what's the problem?"

The mother says, "It's my daughter, Darla. She keeps getting these cravings, she's putting on weight and is sick most mornings."

The doctor gives Darla a good examination, then turns to the mother and says, "Well, I don't know how to tell you this, but your Darla is pregnant. About three months would be my guess."

The mother says, "Pregnant?! She can't be, she has never, ever been alone with a man! Have you, Darla?"

Darla says, "No, Mother! I've never even kissed a man!"

The doctor walks over to the window and just stares out it. About five minutes pass, and finally the mother says, "Is there something wrong out there, doctor?"

The doctor replies, "No, not really. It's just that the last time anything like this happened, a star appeared in the East and three wise men came over the hill. I'll be damned if I'm going to miss it this time!"

When God Visited Earth

God is tired—worn out. So he speaks to St. Peter, "You know, I need a vacation. Got any suggestions where I should go?"

St. Peter thinks for a bit, then nods his head and says, "How about Jupiter? It's nice and warm there this time of the year."

God shakes his head before saying, "No, too much gravity. You know how that hurts my back."

"Hmmm," St. Peter reflects. "Well, how about Mercury?"

"No way!" says God. "It's way too hot for me there!"

"I've got it!" St. Peter says, his face lighting up. "How about going down to Earth for your vacation?"

Chuckling, God remarks, "Are you kidding? Two thousand years ago I went there, had an affair with some nice Jewish girl, and they're still talking about it! Hell, they even celebrate every December."

CHAPTER SEVEN

A Politically (In)Correct
Happy Holiday

Whiskey!

An American congressman was once asked about his attitude toward whiskey.

"If you mean the demon drink that poisons the mind, pollutes the body, desecrates family life and inflames sinners, then I'm against it. But if you mean the elixir of Christmas cheer, the shield against winter chill, the taxable potion that puts needed funds into public coffers to comfort little crippled children, then I'm for it. That is my position, and I will not compromise."

A Politically Correct Holiday Greeting

Best wishes for an environmentally conscious, socially responsible, low stress, non-addictive, gender neutral, winter solstice holiday, practiced within the most joyous traditions of the religious persuasion of your choice, but with respect for the religious persuasion of others as well as those who choose not to practice a religion at all; plus…a fiscally successful, personally fulfilling, medically uncomplicated recognition of the generally accepted calendar year, but not without due respect for the calendars of choice of other cultures whose contributions have helped make our society great, and without regard to the race, creed, color, religion or sexual preference of the wishers and wishees.

Disclaimer: this greeting is subject to clarification or withdrawal. It implies no promise by the wisher to actually implement any of the wishes for her/himself or others and no responsibility for any unintended emotional stress these greetings may bring to those not caught up in the holiday spirit.

> **Q:** Why is it the mentally ill don't send Christmas cards?
>
> **A:** Because they're too busy on their knees praying.

There's a Fly in My Champagne

A multi-national company held a reception to celebrate Christmas. The waiter gave each guest a glass of champagne, but on inspection, each guest noticed that his glass contained a fly. So what did each one do?

The Swede asked for new champagne in the same glass.

The Englishman demanded to have new champagne in a new glass.

The Finn picked out the fly out and drank the champagne.

The Russian drank the champagne, fly and all.

The Chinese ate the fly but left the champagne.

The Israeli caught the fly and sold it to the Chinese.

The Italian drank two-thirds of the champagne and then demanded to have a new glass.

The Norwegian took the fly and went off to fish.

The Irishman ground the fly and mixed it in the champagne, which he then donated to the Englishman.

The American sued the restaurant and claimed $50 million in compensation.

The Scotsman grabbed the fly by the throat and shouted, "Now spit out all that you swallowed!"

Office Party Memos

To: All employees

From: Patty Lewis, Human Resources Director

Date: November 1

Re: Gala Christmas Party

I'm happy to inform you that the company Christmas party will take place on December 23, starting at noon in the private function room at Bill's Steak House. There will be a cash bar and plenty of food! We'll have a small band playing traditional carols… feel free to sing along. And don't be surprised if our CEO shows up dressed as Santa Claus! A Christmas tree will be lit at 1:00 pm. Exchange of gifts among employees can be done at that time; however, to make the giving of gifts easy for everyone's pockets, no gift should be over $10.00. This gathering is for employees only!

Our CEO will make a special announcement during the party!

Merry Christmas to you and your family,

Patty

To: All employees
From: Patty Lewis, Human Resources Director
Date: November 2
Re: Gala Holiday Party

In no way was yesterday's memo intended to exclude our Jewish employees. We recognize that Hanukkah is an important holiday that often coincides with Christmas, though unfortunately not this year. However, from now on, we're calling our gathering a "holiday party."

The same clarification applies to any other employees who are not Christians and to those still celebrating Reconciliation Day. There will be no Christmas tree and no Christmas carols will be sung. We will have other types of music for your enjoyment.

Happy now?

Happy Holidays to you and your family,

Patty

To: All employees
From: Patty Lewis, Human Resources Director
Date: November 3
Re: Holiday Party

Regarding the note I received from a member of Alcoholics Anonymous requesting a non-drinking table, you didn't sign your name. I'm happy to accommodate this request, but if I put a sign on a table that reads "AA Only," you wouldn't be anonymous anymore. How am I supposed to handle this? Somebody?

And sorry, but forget about the gift exchange—no gifts are allowed because the union members feel that $10.00 is too much money and the executives believe $10.00 is a little chintzy.

Patty

To: All employees
From: Patty Lewis, Human Resources Director
Date: November 4
Re: Generic Party

What a diverse group we are! I've arranged for members of Weight Watchers to sit farthest from the dessert buffet, and pregnant women will get the table closest to the restrooms.

Gays are allowed to sit with each other. Lesbians do not have to sit with gay men; each group will have their own table. Yes, there will be flower arrangement for the gay men's table. To the person asking permission to cross dress, Bill's Steak House asks that no cross-dressing be allowed, apparently because of concerns about confusion in the restrooms. Sorry.

We will have booster seats for short people.

Low-fat food will be available for those on a diet.

I am sorry to report that we cannot control the amount of salt used in the food. The manager at Bill's suggests that people with high blood pressure taste a bite first.

There will be fresh "low sugar" fruits as dessert for diabetics, but the restaurant cannot supply "no sugar" desserts. Sorry!

Did I miss anything?!?!?

Patty

To: All f*cking employees

From: Patty Lewis, Human Resources Director

Date: November 5

Re: The F*cking Party

I've had it with you vegetarian pricks!!! We're going to keep this party at Bill's Steak House whether you like it or not, so you can sit quietly at the table farthest from the "grill of death," as you so quaintly put it, and you'll get your f*cking salad bar, including organic tomatoes. But you know, tomatoes have feelings, too. They scream when you slice them. I've heard them scream. I'm hearing them scream right NOW!

The rest of you f*cking weirdos can kiss my ass. I hope you all have a rotten holiday!

Drive drunk and die!

The B*tch from H*ll!!!

To: All employees

From: Maggie Bishop, Acting Human Resources Director

Date: November 6

Re: Patty Lewis and Holiday Party

I'm sure I speak for all of us in wishing Patty Lewis a speedy recovery, and I'll continue to forward your cards to her.

In the meantime, management has decided to cancel our Holiday Party and give everyone the afternoon of the 23rd off with full pay.

Happy Holidays!

Maggie

Atheist Celebrations

An atheist complained to a friend, "Christians have their special holidays, such as Christmas and Easter; and Jewish folks celebrate their holidays, such as Hanukkah and Passover. Every religion has its holidays. But we atheists have no recognized national holidays. It's unfair discrimination."

Q: Why is Christmas just like a day at the office?

A: You do all the work, and the fat guy in the suit gets all the credit.

His friend replied, "Well, why don't you celebrate April First?"

Italian Night Before Christmas

'Twas the night before Christmas,
Da whole house was mella.
Not a creature was stirrin';
I had a gun unda da pilla.

When up on da roof,
I heard somethin' pound.
I sprung to da window,
Screamed, "YO! Keep it down!"

When what to my wonderin'
Eyes should appear,
But da Don of all elfs,
And eight friggin' reindeer!

Wit' slicked-back black hair
And a silk red suit,
Don Kristopher was here,
And he brought da loot!

Wit' a crack of da whip
And a yank on da reins,
He cursed and he shouted
And called dem by name:

"Yo Tony, yo Frankie,
Yo Vinny, yo Vito,
Ay Joey, ay Paulie,
Ay Pepe, ay Guido!"

As I drew out my gun
And hid by da bed,
He flew troo da winda
And slapped me 'side da head.

"What da heck you doin'
Pullin' a gun on da Don?
Now all you're gettin' is coal,
You friggin' moron!"

Den pointin' a fat finga
Right unda my nose,
He twisted his pinky ring,
And up da chimney he rose.

He sprang to his sleigh,
Obscenities screamin',
Away dey all flew,
Before he troo dem a beatin'.

Den I heard him yell out,
What I did least expect,
"Merry friggin' Christmas to all,
And yous better show some respect!"

Differences Between Conservatives/Republicans and Liberals/Democrats

1. Conservatives say "Merry Christmas!" Liberals say "Happy Holidays!"

2. Republicans help the poor during the holidays by sending $50 to the Salvation Army. Democrats help the poor by giving $50, one dollar at a time, to panhandlers on the street.

3. Liberals get back at the Conservatives on their Christmas list by giving them fruitcake. Conservatives re-wrap it and re-gift it.

4. Democrats let their kids open all their gifts on Christmas Eve. Republicans make their kids wait until Christmas morning.

5. When toasting the holidays, Conservatives ask for eggnog or mulled wine. Liberals ask for a "Bud."

6. When not in stores, Republicans shop from a catalog. Democrats watch for "incredible TV offers" on late night television.

7. Liberals do much of their shopping at Target and Walmart. So do Conservatives, but they don't admit it.

8. Republicans parents have no problem buying toy guns for their kids. Democrats refuse to do so. That is why their kids pretend to shoot each other with dolls.

9. Liberals' favorite Christmas movie is *Miracle on 34th Street*. Conservatives' favorite Christmas movie is *It's a Wonderful Life*. Far-right Conservatives' favorite Christmas movie is *Die Hard*.

10. Republicans wear wide red ties and green sports jackets during the festive season. Democrats do too, all year-round.

11. Most Conservatives try, at least once, enclosing indulgent, wretchedly maudlin form letters about their family in their Christmas cards. Public ridicule from Liberals usually discourages them from doing it again.

12. Democrats' favorite Christmas carol is "Deck the Halls." Young Democrats' favorite Christmas carol is "Grandma Got Run Over by a Reindeer." Republicans' favorite Christmas carol is "White Christmas." Young Republicans' favorite Christmas carol is "White Christmas."

13. Cheapskate Conservatives buy an artificial Christmas tree. Tight-fisted Liberals buy a real tree, but they wait until the week before Christmas when the lots lower their prices.

14. Democrat men like to watch hockey while the women fix holiday meals. On this, Republican men are in full agreement.

15. Conservatives first began thinking like Conservatives when they stopped believing in Santa Claus. Liberals became Liberals because they never stopped believing in Santa Claus.

Unhappy Wife

An Englishman, an Irishman and a Scotsman were in the pub deciding what they were going to buy for their wives for Christmas.

The Englishman said, "I'm going to buy my wife a necklace and a scarf. That way, if she doesn't like the necklace, she can wear the scarf on top; she won't be embarrassed, I won't be embarrassed, and we'll have a happy Christmas."

Next it was the Scotsman's turn. "I'm going to buy my wife a bracelet and some long gloves," he said. "That way, if she doesn't like the bracelet, she can wear the gloves on top; she won't be embarrassed, I won't be embarrassed, and we'll have a happy Christmas."

Then they asked the Irishman what he was going to buy. "Well," he said, "I'm going to buy my wife a bright red hat and a vibrator. If she doesn't like the hat, she can go f*ck herself."

The Politically Correct Christmas

On the 12th day of the Eurocentrically imposed midwinter festival, my significant other in a consenting adult, monogamous relationship gave to me:

- twelve males reclaiming their inner warrior through ritual drumming
- eleven pipers piping (plus the 18-member pit orchestra made up of members in good standing of the Musicians Equity Union, as called for in their union contract even though they will not be asked to play a note)

> *Q:* What's Christmas called in England?
> *A:* Yule Britannia!

- ten melanin-deprived, testosterone-poisoned scions of the patriarchal ruling class system leaping
- nine persons engaged in rhythmic self-expression
- eight economically disadvantaged female persons stealing milk products from enslaved Bovine Americans

- seven endangered swans swimming on federally protected wetlands
- six enslaved Fowl Americans producing stolen animal products
- five golden symbols of culturally sanctioned domestic incarceration

(Note: After members of the Animal Liberation Front threatened to throw red paint at my computer, the calling birds, French hens, turtle doves and partridge have been reintroduced to their native habitat. To avoid further animal enslavement, the remaining gift package has been revised.)

- four hours of recorded whale songs
- three deconstructionist poets
- two Sierra Club calendars printed on recycled processed tree carcasses, and
- one spotted owl activist chained to an old-growth pear tree.

Merry Christmas. Happy Hanukkah. Good Kwanzaa. Blessed Yule. Happy Holidays!*†

*Unless otherwise prohibited by law.

† Unless, of course, you are suffering from Seasonally Affected Disorder (SAD). If this be the case, please substitute this gratuitous call for celebration with the suggestion that you have a thoroughly adequate day.

Christmas Carols for the Psychiatrically Challenged

- Schizophrenia: "Do You Hear What I Hear?"
- Multiple Personality Disorder: "We Three Kings Disoriented Are"
- Borderline Personality Disorder: "Thoughts of Roasting in an Open Fire"
- Dementia: "I Think I'll Be Home For Christmas"
- Narcissism: "Hark! The Herald Angels Sing (About Me)"
- Passive aggressive behavior: "On the first day of Christmas, My true love gave to me (and then took it all away)..."
- Mania: "Deck the Halls and Walls and House and Lawn and Streets and Stores and Office and Town"
- Paranoia: "Santa Claus is Coming to Get Me"
- Depression: "Silent anhedonia, Holy anhedonia. All is calm, All is pretty lonely..."
- Obsessive Compulsive Disorder: "Jingle bell, jingle bell, jingle bell rock, Jingle bell, jingle bell, jingle bell rock, Jingle bell, jingle bell, jingle bell rock, Jingle bell, jingle bell, jingle bell rock, Jingle bell, jingle bell, jingle bell rock, Jingle bell, jingle bell, jingle bell rock, Jingle bell, jingle bell, jingle bell rock, Jingle bell, jingle bell..."

CHAPTER EIGHT

'Tis the Season

Hang Your Stockings

'Twas the night before Christmas,
And all through the house,
Not a creature was stirring,
Not even a mouse.

The stockings were hung
By the chimney with care;
They'd been worn all week
And needed the air.

Christmas Generosity

A woman was chatting with her next-door neighbor a couple of weeks before Christmas. "I feel really good today. I started out this morning with an act of unselfish generosity. I gave a 20-dollar bill to a bum."

"You gave a bum 20 whole dollars? That's a lot of money to just give away. What did your husband say about it?"

"Oh, he thought it was the proper thing to do. He said, 'Thanks.'"

Rich People Whims

Once upon a time, there was a fellow who was down on his luck. As he was looking through the classifieds, he saw an intriguing ad offering a $10 million reward to the person who could find and retrieve, intact, something called a "tis bottle." Having nothing to lose, he decided to call the man who placed the ad.

"I absolutely must have this bottle, and there are only three surviving in the world," the wealthy man tells him. "One is in the heart of the deepest jungle; one is at the bottom of the coldest, darkest sea; and one is at the top of the highest mountain. I will pay your expenses for however long it takes to bring me one of these bottles, as well as giving you the 10 million dollars."

Q: Why are Christmas trees like bad knitters?
A: Both drop their needles.

Being an adventurous fellow, he decides to accept the offer. First, he decides to try the jungle. He studies for months to prepare, and when he is ready, he gathers a retinue of guides and hunters to go with him and sets out to get the bottle. Into the jungle he goes, and after many close calls and much loss of life, he finds the bottle.

As he is on his way out of the jungle with the bottle well packed and padded, he is attacked by a tiger, and not only is he badly mauled, but the box with the tis bottle goes flying, and both box and bottle shatter.

It takes some time for him to recover from his injuries, but when he's well enough, he begins preparations to retrieve the bottle at the bottom of the sea. He takes diving lessons, hires the newest and best deep-sea diving equipment and crew, and takes to the sea. With little trouble they manage to get the bottle, but on the way up, they are attacked by sharks and have to rush the rest of the way to the surface. The fellow not only gets the bends, but also, the bottle falls and breaks on the boat deck in the commotion of getting out of the water and tending to shark bites.

Q: What do you get if you cross an apple with a Christmas tree?

A: A pineapple.

More time in the hospital later, recovering slowly, he's more determined than ever to get the third and final bottle. He spends over a year learning mountain climbing and survival, becoming accustomed to low oxygen and heights, and developing the ultimate shatter-proof container for the bottle. He hires a crew of experienced guides and begins his climb. By the time they reach the top, they're low on supplies, weak and frostbitten, but the fellow will not give up. The bottle is packed and secured, and the group begins the descent. When they reach the bottom of the mountain, the fellow again has to spend time in the hospital recovering from his injuries, but he keeps the bottle with him and in sight at all times.

Finally, he's ready to present it to the wealthy man and collect his reward. He goes to the man's house, carefully unpacks the tis bottle and hands it over.

The wealthy man inspects it joyfully, and when he's satisfied it's the right bottle, hands the fellow a check for $10 million. "Thank you and good day, sir," he says, moving to close the door.

"Wait!" the fellow cries. "I was attacked by wild animals, suffered the bends and lost fingers and toes for this bottle. I've spent years looking for it, and almost as long in the hospital recovering from trying to get it. Aren't you going to tell me why it's so precious and what it's for?"

"Um, it's a little embarrassing, actually. Why don't you just take the money and go?"

"I'm not leaving here until you tell me what this bottle is for!" shouts the fellow.

With a sigh, the wealthy man motions for the fellow to follow him. They go into the back of the house, and the man presses a hidden button to reveal a secret door. Behind the door is a small room with another door behind a strong gate. The wealthy man unlocks the gate, unlocks the door and opens the heavy vault door behind it. Inside the vault are hundreds of bottles lined up neatly, wall to wall and floor to ceiling, with one vacant spot labeled "tis." Gently the man places the bottle in its spot and declares, "There you go."

"Oh, come on," the fellow replies. "There has to be more to it than that."

With a sigh, the man picks up a delicate, padded mallet that hangs nearby and gently begins striking the bottles, and a tune emerges: "'Tis the season to be jolly…"

Carol Singer

One Christmas Eve, Freda went carol singing. She knocked on the door of a house and began to sing.

A man with a violin in his hand came to the door. Within half a minute, tears were streaming down his face!

Freda went on singing for half an hour, every carol she knew—and some she didn't. At last she stopped. "I understand," she said softly. "You are remembering your happy childhood Christmas days. You're a sentimentalist!"

"No," the man sniveled, "I'm a musician!"

Plan Ahead

It was Christmas and the judge was in a merry mood as he asked the prisoner, "What are you charged with?"

"Doing my Christmas shopping early," replied the defendant.

"That's no offense," said the judge. "How early were you doing this shopping?"

"Before the store opened."

Two Blondes

There were two blondes who went deep into the frozen forest searching for a Christmas tree. After hours of subzero temperatures and a few close calls with hungry wolves, one blonde turned to the other and said, "I'm chopping down the next tree I see. I don't care whether it's decorated or not!"

My Next Christmas Card

To all my friends who sent me best wishes last year for Christmas, it did f*ck all. For next Christmas, could you please send money, alcohol or gas gift cards? Cheers!

Flying Home

A young man was heading home to spend Christmas with his parents. When he got to the airline counter, he presented his ticket to Chicago. He then gave the agent his luggage and said, "I'd like you to send my red suitcase to Bermuda and my green suitcase to London."

"I'm sorry, sir, but we can't do that," replied the confused agent.

"Really?" replied the man. "Well, I'm very relieved to hear you say that, because that's exactly what you did to my luggage last year!"

Q: What do monkeys sing at Christmas?

A: Jungle bells, jungle bells...

Top 20 Ways to Spoil Your
Roommate's Christmas

20. Claim you were a Christmas tree in your former life. If s/he tries to bring one into the room, scream bloody murder and thrash on the floor.

19. Wear a Santa suit all the time. Deny you're wearing it.

18. Sit in a corner in the fetal position rocking back and forth while chanting, "Santa Claus is coming to town, Santa Claus is coming to town..."

17. Hang mistletoe in the doorway. When your roommate enters or leaves the room, plant a wet one on his/her lips.

16. Hang a stocking with your roommate's name on it. Collect coal and sharp objects in it. If s/he asks, say, "You've been very naughty this year."

15. Paint your nose red and wear antlers. Constantly complain about how you never get to join in on the reindeer games.

14. Make conversation out of Christmas carols. (i.e., "You know, I saw mommy kissing Santa Claus underneath the mistletoe last night.")

13. Give your roommate the gifts from the "Twelve Days of Christmas" song.

12. Build a snowman with your roommate and place a hat on its head. When it doesn't come to life, cry hysterically, "It didn't work!"

11. Whip your roommate while screaming, "Now Dasher, now Dancer, now Prancer and Vixen," etc.

10. Tear down all of your roommate's Christmas decorations, yelling, "Bah humbug!"

9. Wake up every morning screaming, "Ghost of Christmas Future, please have mercy on my soul!"

8. Pin a poinsettia to your lapel.

7. Put on a fake white beard and insist that all your roommate's friends "give it a yank."

6. Ring jingle bells at all hours of the day, saying, "Every time a bell rings, an angel gets his wings."

5. Stand in front of the mirror reciting "How the Grinch Stole Christmas" over and over in your underwear.

4. Smoke mistletoe. Do what comes naturally.

3. Watch your roommate when s/he is sleeping. When s/he wakes up, sing, "He sees you when you're sleeping…"

2. Steal a life-size nativity scene and display it in your room. When your roommate asks, tell him/her, "I had to let them stay here, there's no room at the inn."

1. When your roommate goes to the bathroom, rearrange his/her possessions. Tell him/her that Santa's elves must have done it.

Diary of a New Snow Shoveler

December 8:

It started to snow at 6:00 pm. It's the first snow of the season and the wife and I took our cocktails and sat for hours by the window watching the huge, soft flakes drift down from heaven. It looked like a Grandma Moses print. So romantic we felt like newlyweds again. I love snow!

December 9:

We woke to a beautiful blanket of snow covering every inch of the landscape. What a fantastic sight! Can there be a more lovely place in the whole world? Moving here was the best idea I've ever had. Shoveled for the first time in years and felt like a boy again. I did both our driveway and the sidewalks. This afternoon the snowplow came along and covered up the sidewalks and closed in the driveway, so I got to shovel again. What a perfect life.

December 12:

The sun has melted all our lovely snow. Such a disappointment. My neighbor tells me not to worry, that we'll definitely have a white Christmas. No snow on Christmas would be awful! Bob says we'll have so much snow by the end of winter that I'll never want to see snow again. I don't think that's possible. Bob is such a nice man; I'm glad he's our neighbor.

December 14:

Snow, lovely snow! Eight inches last night. The temperature dropped to minus 20. The cold makes everything sparkle so. The wind took my breath away, but I warmed up shoveling the driveway and sidewalks. This is the life! The snowplow came back this afternoon and buried everything again. I didn't realize I would have to do quite this much shoveling, but I'll certainly get back into shape this way. I wish I wouldn't huff and puff so.

December 15:

There are 20 inches in the forecast. I sold my van and bought a 4x4 Blazer. Bought snow tires for the wife's car and two extra shovels. Stocked the freezer. The wife wants a wood stove in case the electricity goes out. I think that's silly. We aren't in Alaska, after all.

December 16:

Ice storm instead of snow this morning. Fell on my ass in the driveway putting down salt. Hurt like hell. The wife laughed for an hour, which I think was very cruel. The temperature has been steadily falling all day.

December 17:

Still way below freezing. Roads are too icy to go anywhere. Electricity was off for five hours. Had to pile blankets on to stay warm. Nothing to do but stare at the wife and try not to irritate her. I hate it when she's right.

December 20:

More snow. More shoveling. Took all day. God-damn snowplow came by twice. Tried to find a neighbor kid to shovel, but they all said they're to busy playing hockey. I think they're lying. Bob says I have to shovel or the city will have it done and bill me. I think he's lying.

December 22:

Bob was right about a white Christmas because 13 more inches of white sh*t fell today, and it's so cold it probably won't melt until August. Took me 45 minutes to get all dressed up to go out to shovel and then I had to piss. By the time I got undressed, pissed, and dressed again, I was too tired to shovel. Tried to hire Bob, who has a plow on his truck, for the rest of the winter but he says he's too busy. I think the a**hole is lying.

December 23:

Only two inches of snow today. And it warmed up some. But the wife wanted me to decorate the front of the house this morning—what is she, nuts? Why didn't she tell me to do that a month ago? She says she did, but I think she's damn well lying.

December 24:

Six more inches. Snow packed so hard by snow-plow, I broke the shovel. Thought I was having a heart attack. If I ever catch the son-of-a-b*tch who drives that snowplow, I'll drag him through the snow by his balls. I know he hides around the corner and waits for me to finish shoveling, then comes down the street at a 100 miles an hour and throws snow all over where I've just been! Tonight the wife wanted me to sing Christmas carols with her and open our presents, but I was busy watching for the goddamn snowplow.

December 25:

Merry f*cking Christmas—20 more inches of the f*cking slop tonight. Snowed in. The idea of shovel-ing makes my blood boil. I hate the snow!

Season's Greetings

Money's short,
Times are hard;
Here's your f*cking
Christmas card.

Christmas Military Style

An official staff visit by General Claus is expected at this post on 25 December. The following directives govern activities of all army personnel during the visit.

Not a creature will stir without permission. This includes warrant officers and mice. Soldiers may obtain special stirring permits for necessary administrative action through the Battalion S-1. Officer stirring permits must be obtained through the Deputy, Post Plans and Policy Office.

All personnel will settle in for a long winter's nap by 2200 hours, 24 December. Uniform for the nap will be pajamas—cotton, light weight—and general purpose cap and gown—woodland pattern—with ear flaps in the extended position. Equipment will be drawn from the supply room prior to 1900 hours. While at supply, all personnel will review their personal hand receipts and sign a Cash Collection Voucher, for all missing items. Remember, this is the season of giving.

Q: What happens to you at Christmas?

A: Yule be happy.

Personnel will utilize standard T-ration sugar plums for visions to dance through their heads. Sugar plums are available in T-ration sundry packs and should be eaten with some egg loaf, chopped ham and spice cake to ensure maximum visions are experienced.

Stockings, wool, cushion sole, will be hung by the chimneys with care. Necessary safety precautions will be taken to avoid fires caused by carelessly hung stockings. First sergeants will submit stocking handling plans to staff, with training prior to 0800 hours, 24 December. All leaders will ensure their subordinate personnel are briefed on the safety aspects of stocking hanging.

At first sign of clatter, all personnel will spring from their beds to investigate and evaluate the cause. Immediate action will be taken to tear open the shutters and throw up the window sashes. On order, OPLAN 7-97 (North Pole), para 6-8 (c)(3) takes effect to facilitate shutter tearing and sash throwing. All duty officers will be familiar with procedures and are responsible for seeing that no shutters are torn or sashes thrown in Building 9828 prior to the start of official clatter.

Prior to 0001, date of visit, all personnel possessing Standard Target Acquisition and Night Observation (STANO) equipment will be assigned "wandering eyeball" stations. The staff duty non-commissioned officer will ensure that these stations are adequately manned, even after shutters are torn and sashes are thrown.

The Battalion S-4, in coordination with the National Security Agency and the Motor Pool, will assign one sleigh, miniature, M-24, and eight reindeer, tiny, for use by General Claus. The assigned driver must have a current sleigh operator's license with rooftop permit and evidence of attendance at the winter driving class stamped on his DA Form 348. Driver must also be able to clearly shout, "On Dancer, on Prancer," etc.

General Claus will initially enter Building 9828 through the dayroom. All offices without chimneys will draw chimney simulator, M6A2, for use during the visit. Draw chimney simulator on Form 2765-1, which will be submitted in four copies to the staff prior to 23 December. Personnel will ensure that chimneys are properly cleaned before turn-in at the conclusion of visit.

Personnel will be rehearsed in the shouting of "Merry Christmas and Happy New Year!" or "Happy Christmas to all and to all a good night!" This shout will be given upon termination of the visit. Uniformity of shouting is the responsibility of each section non-commissioner officer in charge.

For the Commander Good, U.B.

Executive Officer

Oops!

An elderly lady spent the afternoon at the mall doing her Christmas shopping and, upon returning to the parking lot, found four males in the act of leaving with her car. She dropped her shopping bags and drew her handgun, proceeding to scream at the top of her lungs, "I have a gun, and I know how to use it! Get out of the car!"

The four men didn't wait for a second threat. They got out and ran like mad. The lady, somewhat shaken, proceeded to load her shopping bags into the back of the car and get into the driver's seat. She was so shaken that she could not get her key into the ignition. She tried and tried, and then she realized why. It was for the same reason she had wondered why there was a football, a Frisbee and two 12-packs of beer in the back seat.

Q: What does Dracula write on his Christmas cards?

A: Best vicious of the season.

A few minutes later, she found her own car parked one row over and five spaces farther down. She loaded her bags into the car and drove to the police station to report her mistake. The sergeant to whom she told the story couldn't stop laughing. He pointed to the other end of the room, where four pale men were reporting a carjacking by a mad, elderly woman described as white, less than five feet tall, with glasses, curly white hair, and carrying a large handgun.

No charges were filed. Moral of the story? If you're going to have a senior moment...make it memorable.

Christmas Travel

Shortly before Christmas, a businessman was anxious to get home. The business trip had been grueling, and he was not in a particularly good mood. The airport loudspeakers blared Christmas carols he was sick of hearing. He thought the decorations were tacky. The worst decoration, he thought, was the plastic mistletoe hung over the luggage scale.

Being in a grumpy mood, he said to the woman at the counter, "You know, even if I weren't married, I wouldn't kiss you."

"That's not what it's there for," said the attendant. "It's so you can kiss your luggage goodbye."

Top 10 Christmas Insults

10. A couple of slates short of a full roof.
9. A few pies short of a holiday.
8. All wax and no wick.
7. Batteries not included.
6. Bright as Alaska in December.
5. Chimney's clogged.
4. Stocking filler as brains.
3. Not the brightest bulb on the Christmas tree.
2. Several nuts over fruitcake minimum.
1. A few presents short of a full sleigh.

Competition

It was just before the Christmas shopping rush when a shopkeeper was dismayed to find a brand-new business much like his own had opened up next door and erected a huge sign that read "Best Deals."

He was horrified when another competitor opened up on his other side and announced its arrival with an even larger sign that read "Lowest Prices."

The shopkeeper was panicked until he got an idea. He put the biggest sign of all over his own shop. It read "Main Entrance."

Shoplifting

A shoplifter was caught red-handed trying to steal a watch from an exclusive jewelry store. "Listen," said the shoplifter to the manager, "I know you don't want any trouble either. What do you say I just buy the watch, and we forget about this? It is Christmas time, after all."

Q: How do sheep greet each other at Christmas?

A: Merry Christmas to ewe.

The manager agreed, "All right, but just because it's Christmas," and wrote up the sales slip.

The crook looked at the slip and said, "This is a little more than I intended to spend. Can you show me something less expensive?"

Top 10 Signs You Bought a Lousy Tree

10. You can hear the surveillance cameras moving as they track you across the room.

9. Someone shows up to collect the drugs hidden in the trunk.

8. It's two feet tall, eight feet wide.

7. Salesman's opening line: "You're not a cop, are you?"

6. It looks suspiciously like a broom handle with a lot of coat hangers.

5. You have to explain what "that thing in the corner" is when guests come over.

4. Each branch has "Duraflame" printed on it.

3. It's very small and says "air freshener" on it.

2. Charlie Brown has a better Christmas tree than yours.

1. The rabid squirrel that lives in it jumps out and attacks your children.

Lights

A customer walked into a store looking for Christmas lights. The sales associate showed her the store's top brand. Wanting to make sure each bulb worked, she asked the store employee to take them out of the box and plug them in. He did, and each one lit up.

"Great!" she said.

He carefully placed the string of lights back in the box. But as he handed it to her, she looked alarmed.

"I don't want this box!" she exclaimed. "It's been opened."

The Police Officer's Christmas

'Twas the night before Christmas,
And throughout the substation,
Not a deputy stirred;
They were all on vacation.

The stockings were hung
On the wall with great care,
Next to some T-shirts
And old underwear.

I was working the night shift,
Compiling stats,
Answering the phone,
And feeding the rat.

When all of a sudden
There arose such a clatter,
I leapt from my desk
To see what was the matter!

I opened the door
With a creak and a crick,
And saw a jolly, red fat man
I knew must be St. Nick.

I had seen his picture
A time or two,
He was wanted:
Article 27: Section 342.

I threw open the door
And commanded him "Freeze!
Put your hands on you head,
And get down on your knees."

But he turned and he ran,
Up the chimney he flew,
With me in pursuit,
Toward Booth Street, I knew.

When we got to the roof,
Santa made for his sleigh,
Throwing down toys
And blocking my way.

As I got to the peak,
He threw down some crack,
I slipped and I fell,
Landing flat on my back.

To my front I was faced
With a toy M-1 tank,
And Pink Power Rangers
Covering my flank.

"On Dasher, on Dancer!"
He cried loud and clear.
Then I got off three rounds
And dropped the lead deer.

And I heard Santa say,
As he sailed into the blue,
"Merry Christmas to all!
My lawyers will sue!"

Top 10 Signs You're Not Getting a Christmas Bonus

10. Co-workers refer to you as "the ghost of unemployment future."

9. The last time you saw your boss was when he testified against you at the embezzlement trial.

8. On your door, you find a lovely wreath of pink slips.

7. What you call "my new office," everybody else calls "the supply closet."

6. Your Christmas card from your boss says, "Don't let the door hit you on the way out."

5. You keep getting memos reminding you that employees are required to wear pants.

4. When your boss came over for Thanksgiving, he was crushed under an avalanche of stolen office supplies.

3. Whenever you ask for a raise, a guy shows up at your house and breaks your jaw.

2. In your most recent performance evaluation, the word "terrible" appeared 78 times.

1. You're the starting goaltender for the Toronto Maple Leafs.

Some Musical Christmas Advice

Make out your "Chopin Liszt" early, before "Debussy" season, when you have time to check out some "Verdi" good bargains, can still get gifts "Faure" good price, not have to "Handel" large crowds and have time to give "Bach" things you decide you don't want.

Boxing Day Sale

It was the morning of December 26, and rumors of a big sale (and some advertising in the local paper) were the main reason for the long line that had formed in front of one particular store by 8:30, the day's special opening time.

A small man pushed his way to the front of the line, only to be pushed back amid loud and colorful curses. On the man's second attempt, he was punched square in the jaw and then knocked around a bit before being pushed to the back of the line again. As he got up and dusted himself off, he

Q: What do angry mice send to each other at Christmas?
A: Cross mouse cards.

said to the person next to him in the line, "That does it! If they hit me one more time, I won't open the store!"

CHAPTER NINE

Mom and Dad at Christmas

Turkey Mom

Just before Christmas, the holding pen was abuzz as Mother Turkey scolded her younger birds. "You turkeys are always into mischief," she gobbled. "If your grandfather could see the things you do, he'd turn over in his gravy."

Anything Broken?

John was tasked with bringing the Christmas decorations up from the basement to start decorating the house and tree.

During one trek up the stairs, heavily laden with boxes, he slipped and luckily only fell about two steps before landing square on his behind.

His wife heard the noise and yelled, "What was that thump?"

"I just fell down the stairs," he explained.

"Anything broken?" she asked.

John replied, "No, I'm fine."

There was just a slight pause before his wife said, "No, I meant my decorations—are any of them broken?"

Keep Calm, Monica

It was December 20, the mall was packed and there was one harried woman pushing a cart that contained a little girl who was alternately bellowing and whining. As they passed the toy section, the little girl asked for nearly everything in sight. When the woman told her she couldn't have any new toys that day, the little girl began to scream. The woman got in the check-out line and kept repeating softly, "Don't get excited, Monica; don't scream, Monica; don't be upset, Monica; don't yell, Monica; keep calm, Monica."

A woman standing next to her said, "I couldn't help noticing how patient you are with little Monica!"

The mother replied, "I'm Monica!"

A Car for Christmas

Danny had recently passed his driving test and decided to ask his clergyman father if there was any chance of his getting a car for Christmas, which was yet some months away.

"Okay," said his father, "I tell you what I'll do. If you can get your grades up to A's and B's, study your bible and get your hair cut, I'll consider the matter very seriously."

A couple of months later Danny again brought up the subject with his father, who said, "I'm really impressed by your commitment to your studies. Your grades are excellent, and the work you have put into your bible studies is very encouraging.

However, I have to say I'm very disappointed that you haven't had your hair cut yet.

Danny was a smart young man who was never lost for an answer. "Look, Dad. In the course of my bible studies I've noticed in the illustrations that Moses, John the Baptist, Samson and even Jesus had long hair."

"Yes, that's true," replied his father. "But did you also notice they walked wherever they went?"

Watch What You Say...

A family of three was getting ready to have company over for Christmas dinner. Bored, the little boy, Johnny, walked outside the house and overheard this part of a conversation between his neighbors: "Put your penis in my vagina."

Johnny returned to the house and went to find his dad. "Daddy, what's a penis and vagina?"

"Well, Johnny, a penis is a coat and a vagina is a hat," his father explained, not wanting to get into the real meanings right then.

Q: Do you know what it is like to put up 1500 Christmas lights on the roof of a house?

A: The kids are giving two to one odds I'm gonna come down the chimney before Santa Claus does.

Wandering around the house, Johnny reached his mother in the kitchen cutting the turkey. All of a sudden, she cut herself and yelled, "F*CK!"

Curious, Johnny asked her the meaning.

"Well, Johnny, f*ck is a way to cut a turkey."

Next, Johnny went back to his father, who was now in the bathroom shaving. He cut himself and yelled, "Sh*t!"

"Daddy, what's sh*t?"

"Well Johnny, sh*t is shaving cream."

Just then their expected company rang the doorbell, leaving Johnny to answer the door. Wanting to sound mature, he used the words he had just learned: "Welcome to our house, ladies and gentlemen. If you would please hand me your penises and vaginas, my father is wiping sh*t off his face and my mother is f*cking the turkey."

A Christmas Visit

A man in Montreal calls his son in Vancouver on December 23 and says, "I hate to ruin your Christmas, but I have to tell you that your mother and I are divorcing; 30 years of misery is enough."

"Dad, what are you talking about?!" the son exclaims.

"We can't stand the sight of each other any longer," the father says. "We're sick of each other, and I'm sick of talking about this, so you can call your sister in Aberdeen and tell her."

Frantic, the son calls his sister, who explodes over the phone. "Like hell they're getting divorced!" she shouts. "I'll take care of this."

She calls home immediately and screams at her father, "You are NOT getting divorced. Don't do a single thing until I get there. I'm calling my brother back, and we'll both be there tomorrow. Until then, don't do a thing! DO YOU HEAR ME?!" And she hangs up.

The man hangs up his phone and turns to his wife. "Okay," he says, "they're coming for Christmas—and they're paying their own way."

Christmas Dinner with Mom

Brian invited his mother over for Christmas dinner. During the course of the meal, she couldn't help but notice how beautiful Brian's roommate, Stephanie, was. She had long been suspicious of a relationship between Brian and Stephanie, and finally meeting the girl had only made her more curious. Over the course of the evening, while watching the two interact, she started to become convinced that there was more between Brian and Stephanie than met the eye.

Reading his mom's thoughts, Brian volunteered, "I know what you must be thinking, but I assure you, Stephanie and I are just roommates."

About a week later, Stephanie came to Brian and said, "Ever since your mother came to dinner, I've been unable to find the beautiful silver gravy ladle. You don't suppose she took it, do you?"

Brian said, "Well, I doubt it, but I'll send her an e-mail just to be sure."

So he sat down and wrote, "Dear Mom, I'm not saying that you did take the gravy ladle from the house; I'm not saying that you did not take the gravy ladle. But the fact remains that it has been missing ever since you were here for dinner. Love, Brian."

The next day, Brian received an e-mail back from his mother that read, "Dear Son, I'm not saying that you do sleep with Stephanie; I'm not saying that you do not sleep with Stephanie. But the fact remains that if Stephanie was sleeping in her own bed, she would have found the gravy ladle by now. Love, Mom."

Christmas Stuffing

This is a story about a couple who had been happily married for years. The only friction in their marriage was the husband's habit of farting loudly every morning when he awoke. The noise would wake his wife and the smell would make her eyes water and leave her gasping for air.

Every morning she would plead with him to stop ripping them off because it was making her sick. He told her he couldn't stop it and that it was perfectly natural. She told him to see a doctor; she was concerned that one day he would blow his guts out. The years went by and he continued to rip them off.

Husband defined: a man who buys his football tickets four months in advance and waits until December 24 to do his Christmas shopping.

Then one Christmas morning as she was preparing the turkey for dinner and he was upstairs sound asleep, she looked at the bowl where she had put the turkey neck, gizzard, liver and all the spare parts.

A malicious thought came to her. She took the bowl and went upstairs to where her husband was sound asleep. Gently folding back the bed covers, she pulled back the elastic waistband of his underpants and emptied the bowl of turkey guts into his shorts.

Sometime later she heard her husband waken with his usual trumpeting, which was followed by a blood-curdling scream and the sound of frantic footsteps as he ran into the bathroom.

She could hardly control herself as she rolled on the floor laughing. After years of torture, she reckoned she had got him back pretty good. About 20 minutes later, her husband came downstairs in his blood-stained underpants with a look of horror on his face. She bit her lip as she asked him what was the matter.

He said, "Honey, you were right. All these years you have warned me, and I didn't listen to you."

"What do you mean?" asked his wife.

"Well, you always told me that one day I would end up farting my guts out, and today it finally happened. But by the grace of God, some Vaseline and these two fingers, I think I got most of them back in."

Home for the Holidays

My son Mark was only 5 feet, 8 inches tall when he left for college in the fall. His first visit home was for the Christmas holidays.

When he got off the plane, I was stunned at how much taller he looked. Measuring him at home,

I discovered he now stood at 5 feet, 11 inches. My son was as surprised as I. "Couldn't you tell by your clothes that you'd grown?" I asked him.

"Since I've been doing my own laundry," he replied, "I just figured everything had shrunk."

Lost and Found

A man approached a very beautiful woman in the large shopping mall that was packed with holiday shoppers and said, "I've lost my wife here in the mall. Can you talk to me for a couple of minutes?"

"Why?"

"Because every time I talk to a beautiful woman, my wife appears out of nowhere."

What a Boy Wants for Christmas

David remembers accompanying his father out shopping in the toy department of Macy's one Christmas Eve.

His dad said, "What a marvelous train set. I'll buy it."

The girl behind the counter looked pleased and murmured, "Great, I'm sure your son will really love it."

His dad looked startled for a second before he recovered himself and said, "Maybe you're right. In that case, I'll take two."

Gift for Dad

'Twas the night before Christmas,
And all through the house,
The kids were all sleeping,
Each quiet as a mouse.

Mom was carrying toys
In her see-through nightgown,
Showing her person
From her middle on down.

When she crept past the crib
Of her little baby boy,
Her youngest and sweetest,
Her pride and her joy.

His eyes opened wide
As he stared from his cot,
And he saw everything,
Including Mom's tw*t.

He didn't even notice
The toys on her lap.
He just asked her, "For who
Is that little fur cap?"

His mother said, "Hush."
And she laughed with delight.
"I think I'll give that
To your father tonight!"

Breasts and Penises

A family is sitting around the supper table. The son asks his father, "Dad, how many kinds of breasts are there?"

The father, surprised, takes a minute before he answers, "Well, son, there are three kinds of breasts. In her twenties, a woman's breasts are like melons, round and firm. In her thirties to forties, they are like pears, still nice but hanging a bit. After fifty, they are like onions."

"Onions?"

"Yes, you see them and they make you cry."

This infuriates the wife and daughter, so the daughter says, "Mom, how many kind of penises are there?"

The mother smiles, looks at her husband and answers, "Well, dear, a man goes through three phases. In a man's twenties, his penis is like an oak, mighty and hard. In his thirties and forties, it is like a birch, flexible but reliable. After his fifties, it is like a Christmas tree."

"A Christmas tree?"

"Yes, dead from the root up, and the balls are there for decoration only.

Backseat Driver

My wife and I get along just great, except that she's a backseat driver second to none. After years of putting up with her pestering, I finally decided

I'd had enough, and as an early Christmas present to myself, I advised her that I would no longer drive with her in the car.

Later that day, on my way home from doing some Christmas shopping at the mall, I heard my cell phone ring as I was merging onto the freeway. It was my wife calling. By chance, she had entered the freeway right behind me.

"Honey," she said, "your turn signal is still on. And put on your lights; it's starting to snow."

Your Father is Drunk (to the tune of "Santa Claus Is Coming to Town")

Oh you better not shout, you better not cry,
You better not pout, I'm tellin' you why,
Daddy's home and I think he's drunk.

He's walkin' real slow, he slurs when he speaks,
I don't even think he's shaved in two weeks,
Daddy's home and boy is he drunk.

He spent most of our money on Johnny Walker Black,
And then he took all of the rest and lost it at the track.
Sooooooo…

You better not shout, you better not cry,
I don't like that look in his eye,
Daddy's home and I think he's—
Daddy's home and boy is he—
Daddy's home and he's really drunk!

Mom's Christmas List

Dear Santa,

I've been a good mom all year. I've fed, cleaned and cuddled my two children on demand, visited the doctor's office more than my doctor has, sold 62 cases of candy bars to raise money to plant a shade tree on the school playground, and figured out how to attach nine patches onto my daughter's Girl Scout sash with staples and a glue gun.

Here is my Christmas list; I have a few items, and I was hoping you could spread my gifts out over several Christmases, since I had to write this letter with my son's red crayon on the back of a receipt in the laundry room between cycles, and who knows when I'll find any more free time in the next 18 years.

First, I'd like a pair of legs that don't ache after a day of chasing kids (in any color except purple, which I already have) and arms that don't flap in the breeze, but are strong enough to carry a screaming toddler out of the candy aisle in the grocery store. I'd also like a waist, since I lost mine somewhere in the seventh month of my last pregnancy.

If you're hauling big ticket items this year, I'd like a car with fingerprint-resistant windows and a radio that plays only adult music; a television that doesn't broadcast any programs containing talking animals; and a closet with a secret compartment behind the shelves where I can hide to talk on the phone.

I could use a talking daughter doll that says, "Yes, Mommy" to boost my parental confidence, along with one potty-trained toddler and two kids who don't fight. I could also use a recording of Tibetan monks chanting, "Don't eat in the living room" and "Take your hands off your brother," because my voice seems to be just out of my children's hearing range.

On the practical side, three pairs of jeans that will zip all the way up without the use of power tools would be useful. And please don't forget the Play-Doh Travel Pack, *the* stocking stuffer this year for mothers of preschoolers. It comes in three fluorescent colors and is guaranteed to crumble on any carpet, making the in-laws' house seem just like mine.

If it's too late to find any of these products, I'd settle for enough time to brush my teeth and comb my hair in the same morning, or the luxury of eating food warmer than room temperature without it being served in a Styrofoam container.

If you don't mind, I could also use a few Christmas miracles to brighten the holiday season. Would it be too much trouble to declare ketchup a vegetable? It would clear my conscience immensely. It would also be nice if you could coerce my children to help around the house without demanding payment as if they were the bosses of an organized crime family; or if my toddler didn't look so cute sneaking downstairs to eat contraband ice cream in his pajamas at midnight.

Well, Santa, the buzzer on the dryer is ringing and my son saw my feet under the laundry room door. I think he wants his crayon back. Have a safe trip, and remember to leave your wet boots by the fire and come in and dry off so you don't catch a cold. Help yourself to the cookies on the table, but please don't eat too many or leave crumbs on the carpet.

Yours always,

A mom

Husband Shopping

Just before Christmas, a company opened a Husband Super Store, where single women could go to choose a husband from among many men. The owners hoped sales would be good at one of the loneliest times of the year for singles. The store was laid out over five floors, with the men increasing in positive attributes as you ascended. The only rules were, once you opened the door to any floor, you HAD to choose a man from that floor. And if you went up a floor, you couldn't go back down except to leave the place, never to return.

So a couple of girlfriends went to the shopping center to find some husbands as the ultimate Christmas present to themselves.

First floor. The door had a sign saying, "These men have jobs and love kids."

The women read the sign and said, "Well that's better than not having a job or not loving kids, but I wonder what's farther up?" So up they went.

Second floor. The sign read, "These men have high-paying jobs, love kids and are extremely good looking."

"Hmmm," said the ladies. "That's pretty good, but I wonder what's farther up?"

Third floor. This sign read, "These men have high-paying jobs, love kids, are extremely good looking and help with the housework."

"Wow!" said the women. "Very tempting." But there was another floor, so farther up they went.

Fourth floor. This door had a sign saying, "These men have high-paying jobs, love kids, are extremely good looking, help with the housework and have a strong romantic streak that includes buying diamonds for Christmas."

"Oh, mercy me!" they cried. "Just think what must be awaiting us farther on!" So up to the fifth floor they went.

Fifth floor. The sign on that door said, "There are no men on this floor. This floor exists solely as proof that women are impossible to please. Thank you for shopping at the Husband Super Store."

To avoid gender bias issues, the store owners opened a New Wives store as well, just across the street. The first floor had wives that love sex. The second floor had wives that love sex and have money. The third through fifth floors were never visited.

⋘ CHAPTER TEN ⋙
Christmas Festivities

Rating Your Christmas Party

If you throw a party, the worst thing you can do is throw the kind of party where your guests call you up the next day to say they had a nice time. Then you'll be expected to throw another great party the next year.

What you should do is throw the kind of party where your guests wake up several days later and call their lawyers to find out if they've been indicted for anything. You want your guests to be so anxious to avoid a recurrence of your party that they immediately start planning parties of their own, a year in advance, just to prevent you from having another one. So, make sure your party reaches the correct Festivity Level.

Festivity Level One: Your guests are chatting amiably with each other, admiring your Christmas-tree ornaments, singing carols around the upright piano, sipping at their drinks and nibbling at hors d'oeuvres.

Festivity Level Two: Your guests are talking loudly—sometimes to each other and sometimes to nobody at all—rearranging your Christmas-tree ornaments, singing "Jingle Bells" around the upright piano, gulping their drinks and wolfing down hors d'oeuvres.

Festivity Level Three: Your guests are arguing violently with inanimate objects, singing "Jingle bells, Batman smells..." gulping other people's drinks, wolfing down Christmas-tree ornaments and placing hors d'oeuvres in the upright piano to see what happens when the little hammers strike them.

(You want to keep your party somewhere around Level Three, unless you rent your home and own firearms, in which case you can go to Level Four.)

Festivity Level Four: Your guests have hors d'oeuvres smeared all over their bodies, are performing a ritual dance around the burning Christmas tree and have consumed all 10 gallons of alcohol at the party. The piano is missing.

The best way to get to Level Four is eggnog. To make eggnog, you'll need rum, whiskey, wine, gin and, if they are in season, eggs. Combine all ingredients in a large, festive bowl. If you use enough alcohol, you won't have to worry about your guests getting salmonella poisoning. Then induce your guests to drink this potent mixture steadily all night.

If your party is successful, the police will knock on your door. If your party is very successful, the police will then lob tear gas through your living-room window. As host, your job is to make sure they don't arrest anybody. Or, if they're dead set on arresting someone, your job is to make sure it isn't you.

The best way to do this is to show a lot of respect for their uniforms and assure them you're not doing anything illegal.

Good Nog

If you see a fat man
Who's jolly and cute,
Wearing a beard
And a red flannel suit,

And if he is chuckling
And laughing away,
While flying around
In a miniature sleigh,

With eight tiny reindeer
To pull him along,
Then let's face it—
Your eggnog's too strong!

Party Aftermath

One Monday morning a mailman is walking the neighborhood on his usual route. As he approaches one of the homes he notices that both cars are in the driveway. His curiosity is cut short by Bob, the homeowner, coming out with a large load of empty beer and liquor bottles. "Wow, looks like you guys had one hell of a party last night," the mailman comments.

Bob, in obvious pain, replies, "Actually, we had the party Saturday night. This is the first I have felt

What I don't like about office Christmas parties is looking for a new job the next day.

like moving since 4:00 AM Sunday morning. We had about 15 couples from around the neighborhood over for some Christmas cheer, and it got a bit wild. Hell, we got so drunk that around midnight we started playing 'Who am I?'."

The mailman doesn't know that game and asks, "How do you play?"

"Well, all the guys go in the bedroom, and we come out one at a time with a sheet covering us and only our privates showing through a hole in the sheet. Then the women try to guess who it is," answers Bob.

The mailman laughs and says, "Damn, I'm sorry I missed that."

"Probably a good thing you did," says Bob. "Your name came up four or five times."

Christmas Turkey

It was Christmas Eve, and at the meat counter at the grocery store, a woman was anxiously looking over the few remaining turkeys in the hope of finding a large one. In desperation, she called over a shop assistant and said, "Excuse me, do these turkeys get any bigger?"

"No, madam," he replied. "They're all dead."

Helpful Holiday Diet Tips

1. If no one sees you eat it, it has no calories.

2. If you drink a diet soda with a candy bar, they cancel each other out.

3. If you eat standing up, it doesn't count.

4. "Stressed" is just "desserts" spelled backwards; therefore, one cures the other.

5. If you eat the food off someone else's plate, it doesn't count.

6. Cookie pieces contain no calories because the process of breakage causes calorie leakage.

7. Food used for medicinal purposes has no calories. This includes any chocolate used for energy, brandy, cheesecake, and Häagen-Dazs ice cream.

8. When eating with someone else, calories don't count if you both eat the same amount.

9. Movie-related food is much lower in calories simply because it is a part of the entertainment experience and not part of one's personal fuel. This includes Milk Duds, popcorn with butter, Junior Mints, Snickers and Gummi Bears.

The Office Party

John woke up after the annual office Christmas party with a pounding headache, cotton-mouthed and utterly unable to recall the events of the preceding evening. After a trip to the bathroom, he made his way downstairs, where his wife put some coffee in front of him. "Louise," he moaned, "tell me what happened last night. Was it as bad as I think?"

"Even worse," she said, her voice oozing scorn. "You made a complete ass of yourself. You succeeded in antagonizing the entire board of directors, and you insulted the president of the company right to his face."

"He's an a**hole," John said. "Piss on him."

"You did," Louise replied, "and he fired you."

"Well, screw him!" said John.

"I did. You're back at work on Monday."

Suicide Savior

It's Christmas party time at work, and there is a man sitting on the railing of the roof, about to jump off.

Suddenly, Santa Claus is standing next to him, holding him by his collar. "What do you think you're doing?" asks Santa.

"I've had enough, and I want to die," says the man. "This morning I was told I was made redundant, and when I called my wife to tell her, she decided to leave me. I won't have the money to pay for the mortgage, and I owe thousands on my credit cards."

"What if you were to wake up tomorrow morning to discover you've got twice what you owe in your bank account, your wife is totally in love with you, and you got promoted and a huge raise at work?" asks Santa.

"Can you really do that for me?" asks the man.

"Just drop your pants and let me give you one, and all your troubles will be over," Santa assures him.

The man has no choice but to accept.

After the deed, Santa asks, "How old are you?"

"I'm 36," says the man, readjusting himself.

"And you still believe all that bullsh*t fairy tale stuff?" asks the big fat man in a red suit.

Very Accommodating Hostess

A New York woman throws a Christmas party. One of the guests is a tall, handsome Texan. "Is there anything I can do for you?" she asks, fluttering her lashes.

"Yes ma'am, I sure could use a piece of ass."

She nods, takes the Texan into the bedroom, removes her clothes and engages him in a steamy session of lovemaking. When they are done, she again asks suggestively, "Now, handsome, is there anything else I can do for you?"

"Well, ma'am," he replies, "I still could use that piece of ass for my drink."

A Christmas Wish

May your stuffing be tasty,
May your turkey be plump,
May your potatoes and gravy
Have never a lump.

May your cakes be delicious,
And your pies take the prize,
And may your Christmas dinner
Stay off your thighs!

You know you've had too much Christmas cheer when...

1. You notice your tie sticking out of your fly.

2. Someone uses your tongue for a coaster.

3. You start kissing the portraits on the wall.

4. You see your underwear hanging from the chandelier.

5. You have to hold on to the floor to keep from sliding off.

6. You strike a match and light your nose.

7. You take off your shoes and wade in the potato salad.

8. You hear someone say, "Call a priest!"

9. You hear a duck quacking and realize it's you.

10. You complain about the small bathroom after emerging from the closet.

11. You refill your glass from the fish bowl.

12. You tell everyone you have to go home...and the party's at your place.

13. You ask for another ice cube and put it in your pocket.

14. You yawn at the biggest bore in the room and realize you're in front of the hall mirror.

15. You pick up a roll and butter your watch.

16. You suggest everyone stand and sing the national budget.

17. You're at the dinner table and you ask the hostess to pass a bedpan.

18. You take out your handkerchief and blow your ear.

19. You tell your best joke to the rubber plant.

20. You realize you're the only one under the coffee table.

Christmas Cake Recipe

For this recipe you'll need the following:

1 cup of water
1 cup of butter
1 cup of sugar
4 large brown eggs
2 cups of dried fruit
1 teaspoon of salt
1 cup of brown sugar
1 tablespoon of lemon juice
1 cup chopped walnuts
1 bottle of whiskey

Sample the whiskey to check for quality. Take a large bowl. Check the whiskey again. To be sure it's the highest quality, pour one level cup and drink. Repeat. Turn on the electric mixer, and beat the butter in a large, fluffy bowl. Add one teaspoon of sugar and beat again. Make sure the whiskey is still okay.

> Christmas is the only birthday party where everybody gets presents except the guy whose birthday it is.

Cry another tup. Tune up the mixer. Beat two eggs and add to the bowl and chuck in the cup of dried fruit. Mix on the turner. If the dried fruit gets stuck in the beaterers, pry it goose with a screwdriver.

Sample the whiskey to check for consistency. Next, sift two cups of salt. Or something. Who cares?

Check the whiskey. Now sift the lemon juice and strain your nuts. Add one table. Spoon the sugar or something. Whatever you can find. Grease the oven. Turn the cake tin to 350°F. Don't forget to beat off the turner. Throw the bowl out the window. Check the whiskey again and go to bed.

Q: Why didn't the skeleton go to the Christmas party?
A: He had no body to go with!

Office Memo

To: All employees
From: Management
Date: December 1
Re: Office conduct during the Christmas season

Effective immediately, employees should keep in mind the following guidelines in compliance with the Federal Revelry Office and Leisure Industry Council (FROLIC):

1. Running aluminum foil through the paper shredder to make tinsel is discouraged.

2. Playing "Jingle Bells" on the push-button phone is forbidden (it runs up an incredible long distance phone bill).

3. Work requests are not to be filed under "Bah humbug."

4. Company cars are not to be used to go over the river and through the woods to Grandma's house.

5. All fruitcake is to be eaten BEFORE July 25.

6. Eggnog will NOT be dispensed in vending machines.

7. In spite of all this, the staff is encouraged to
    have a Happy Holiday.

A Holiday(ing) Turkey

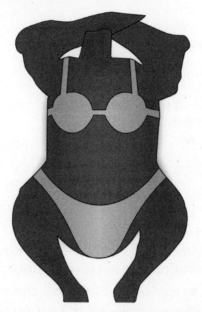

Here is a new way to prepare your Christmas
turkey:

1. Cut out aluminum
    foil in desired shapes
    (see illustration).

2. Arrange the turkey in
    the roasting pan, posi-
    tioning the foil care-
    fully.

3. Roast.

4. Serve. Watch your guests' faces...

Q: What did Dracula say at
the Christmas party?

A: Fancy a bite?

Top 20 Uses for Fruit Cake
(Other than Eating)

20. Use it as a doorstop.

19. Use it as a paper weight.

18. Use it as book ends.

17. Use slices to scrub your pots and pans.

16. Use it as a boat anchor.

15. Use several as bricks in a fireplace.

14. Use it as speed bumps to foil the neighborhood drag racers.

13. One word: pincushion.

12. Send lots to the U.S. Air Force, let troops drop them on the enemy.

11. Give it to the cat for a scratching post.

10. Put it in the backyard to feed the birds and squirrels.

9. Use slices to balance that wobbly kitchen table.

8. Use them instead of sand bags during a flood.

7. Use a couple instead of cement shoes.

6. Use it as a replacement for a Duraflame log.

5. Take it camping with you to use to weigh down the tent.

4. Use slices in your next skeet-shooting competition.

3. Stand on it when you need to change a light bulb.

2. Put it in the back of your car/truck for snow/ice driving.

1. Replaces free weights when you work out.

CHAPTER ELEVEN

Happy Hanukkah!

Hanukkah Visit

Last year, just before Hanukkah, a Jewish grandmother was giving directions to her grown-up grandson, who was coming to visit with his wife. "You come to the front door of the condominium complex. I am in apartment 2B," she said over the phone. "There is a big panel at the door. With your elbow, push button 2B. I will buzz you in. Come inside, and the elevator is on the right. Get in, and with your elbow hit the button for the second floor. When you get out, I am on the left. With your elbow, hit my doorbell."

"Grandma, that sounds easy," replied the grandson, "but why am I hitting all these buttons with my elbow?"

To which she answered, "You're coming to visit empty handed?"

Jewish Mothers

My mother once gave me two sweaters for Hanukkah. The next time I visited, I made sure to wear one.

As I walked in the door, instead of the expected smile, she said to me, "Aaron, what's the matter? You didn't like the other one?"

Chinese Yiddish English

On the fifth day of Hanukkah, which happened to be Christmas day, two elderly Jewish men were sitting in a wonderful deli in New York City frequented almost exclusively by Jews. They were talking amongst themselves in Yiddish—the colorful language of Jews who came over from Eastern Europe.

A Chinese waiter, having been only one year in New York, came up and, in fluent, impeccable Yiddish, asked them if everything was okay and if they were enjoying the holiday.

The Jewish men were dumbfounded. After they paid the bill, they asked the restaurant manager, an old friend of theirs, "Where did your waiter learn such fabulous Yiddish?"

Q: What did the little candle say to the big candle?
A: I'm going out tonight.

The manager looked around and leaned in so no one else could hear and said, "Shhhh. He thinks we're teaching him English."

Stamps at Hanukkah

Mary goes to the post office to buy stamps for her Hanukkah cards. She says to the cashier, "May I have 50 Hanukkah stamps?'

The cashier says, "What denomination?"

Mary says, "Oy vey, has it come to this? Okay, give me six Orthodox, 12 Conservative and 32 Reform."

Rudi the Rabbi

It was Hanukkah, and the people of a tiny village outside Budapest in Hungary were frightened that they may not have any latkes because they had run out of flour.

Rudi, the village rabbi, was called upon to help solve the problem. He said, "Don't worry, you can substitute matzo meal for the flour, and the latkes will be just as delicious."

Sarah looked to her husband and said, "Samuel, do you think it'll work?"

"Of course," Samuel replied. "Everybody knows Rudolph the Rabbi knows grain, dear."

Holy Merger

Continuing the current trend of large-scale mergers and acquisitions, it was announced today at a press conference that Christmas and Hanukkah will merge. An industry source said that the deal had been in the works for about 1300 years.

While details were not available at press time, it is believed that the overhead cost of having 12 days of Christmas and eight days of Hanukkah was becoming prohibitive for both sides. Massive layoffs are expected, with lords a-leaping and maids a-milking being the hardest hit. But by combining forces, we're told, the world will be able to enjoy consistently high-quality service during the Ten Days of Chrismukah, as the new holiday is being called.

As part of the conditions of the agreement, the letters on the dreidel, currently in Hebrew, will be replaced by Latin, thus becoming unintelligible to a wider audience. Also, instead of translating to "A great miracle happened there," the message on the dreidel will be the more generic "Miraculous stuff happens." In exchange, it is believed that Jews will be allowed to use Santa Claus and his vast merchandising resources for buying and delivering their gifts.

One of the sticking points holding up the agreement for at least 300 years was the question of whether Jewish children could leave milk and cookies for Santa even after having eaten meat for dinner. A breakthrough came last year, when Oreos were finally declared to be Kosher. All sides appeared happy about this.

A spokesman for Christmas, Inc., declined to say whether a takeover of Kwanzaa might be in the works as well. He merely pointed out that, were it not for the independent existence of Kwanzaa, the merger between Christmas and Hanukkah might indeed be seen as an unfair cornering of the holiday market. Fortunately for all concerned, he said, Kwanzaa will help to maintain the competitive balance. He then closed the press conference by leading all present in a rousing rendition of "Oy Vey, All Ye Faithful."

Q: Why is a burning candle like being thirsty?
A: Because a little water ends both of them.

Happy Holidays

As the plane taxied into the airport gate, the voice of the captain came on: "Please remain seated with your seatbelt fastened until the plane is at a complete standstill and the seatbelt signs have been turned off.

"To those of you standing in the aisles, we wish you a Happy Hanukkah. To those who have remained in your seats, we wish you a Merry Christmas."

> "Most Texans think Hanukkah is some sort of duck call."
> –*Richard Lewis*

Top 10 Reasons to Like Hanukkah

10. No roof damage from reindeer.
9. There's never a silent night when you're among your Jewish loved ones.
8. If someone screws up getting someone a bad gift, there are seven more days to correct it.
7. Betting Hanukkah gelt (the chocolate coins) on candle races.
6. You can use your fireplace.
5. Playing naked Spin-the-Dreidel.
4. Fun waxy buildup on the menorah.
3. No awkward explanations of virgin birth.
2. Cheer is optional.
1. No Irving Berlin songs.

A Tree for Christmas

Admiring the Christmas trees displayed in his neighbor's windows, Nathan asks his father, "Daddy, can we have a Hanukkah tree?"

"What? No, of course not," says his father.

"Why not?" asks Nathan.

His father replies, "Well, Nathan, because the last time we had dealings with a lighted bush, we spent 40 years in the wilderness."

Compare and Contrast

Stan and John are walking to school one day, and Stan is showing his new iPod to John.

"Where did you get that?" John asks.

"I got it last night for Hanukkah," says Stan.

"What's Hanukkah?" John asks.

"It's a Jewish holiday, where we get presents every night for eight nights, to celebrate the Festival of Lights."

"Wow, I wish we got that!" John exclaims.

Q: How long does it take to burn a candle down?

A: About a wick.

The next day, on the way to school, John runs up to Stan, curious to see what he got, but he sees that Stan is upset. "What's wrong? Where's your present from last night?" asks John.

Stan holds up a ball of crumpled wrapping paper. "It was leftovers night."

Oy, a Letter!

Dear Darling Son,

Happy Hanukkah to you, and please don't worry. I'm just fine, considering I can't breathe or eat. The important thing is that you have a nice holiday, thousands of miles away from your ailing mother. I've sent along my last 10 dollars with this letter, which I hope you'll spend on my grandchildren. God knows their mother never buys them anything nice. They look so thin in their pictures, poor babies.

Thank you so much for the birthday flowers, dear boy. I put them in the freezer so they'll stay fresh for my grave. Which reminds me—we buried Grandma last week. I know she died years ago, but I got to yearning for a good funeral, so Aunt Berta and I dug her up and had the services all over again. I would have invited you, but I know that woman you live with would have never let you come. I bet she's never even watched that videotape of my hemorrhoid surgery, has she?

Well, son, it's time for me to crawl off to bed now. I lost my cane beating off muggers last week, but don't you worry about me. I'm also getting used to the cold since they turned my heat off and am grateful because the frost on my bed numbs the constant pain in my joints. Now don't you even think about sending any more money because I know you need it for those expensive family vacations you take

> A Jewish Santa Claus came down the chimney and said, "Anyone want to buy a present?"

every year. Give my love to my darling grand-babies
and my regards to whatever-her-name-is—the one
with the black roots who stole you screaming from
my bosom.

Love,

Your Mother

The Eight Days of Hanukkah

On the first night of Hanukkah my true love gave
to me,
Lox, bagels and some cream cheese.

On the second night of Hanukkah, my true love
gave to me,
Two kosher pickles and
Lox, bagels and some cream cheese.

On the third night of Hanukkah, my true love
gave to me,
Three pounds of corned beef,
Two kosher pickles and
Lox, bagels and some cream cheese.

On the fourth night of Hanukkah, my true love
gave to me,
Four potato latkes,
Three pounds of corned beef,
Two kosher pickles and
Lox, bagels and some cream cheese.

On the fifth night of Hanukkah, my true love
gave to me,
Five bowls of chicken soup,

Four potato latkes,
Three pounds of corned beef,
Two kosher pickles and
Lox, bagels and some cream cheese.

On the sixth night of Hanukkah, my true love
gave to me,
Six pickled herrings,
Five bowls of chicken soup,
Four potato latkes,
Three pounds of corned beef,
Two kosher pickles and
Lox, bagels and some cream cheese.

On the seventh night of Hanukkah, my true love
gave to me,
Seven noodle kugels,
Six pickled herrings,
Five bowls of chicken soup,
Four potato latkes,
Three pounds of corned beef,
Two kosher pickles and
Lox, bagels and some cream cheese.

On the eighth night of Hanukkah, my true love
gave to me,
Eight Alka-Seltzer tablets,
Seven noodle kugels,
Six pickled herrings,
Five bowls of chicken soup,
Four potato latkes,
Three pounds of corned beef,
Two kosher pickles and
Lox, bagels and some cream cheese.

What to Do on Christmas Eve

'Twas the night before Christmas,
And, being Jews,
My girlfriend and me—
We had nothing to do.

The Gentiles were home,
Hanging stockings with care,
Secure in their knowledge
St. Nick would be there.

But for us, once the Hanukkah
Candles burned down,
There was nothing but boredom
All over town.

The malls and the theaters
Were all closed up tight;
There weren't any concerts
To go to that night.

A dance would have saved us,
Some ballroom or swing,
But we searched through the papers;
There wasn't a thing.

Outside the window
Sat two feet of snow;
With the wind-chill, they said
It was fifteen below.

While all I could do
Was sit there and brood,
My girl saved the night
And called out, "Chinese food!"

So we ran to the closet,
Grabbed hats, mitts and boots
To cover our heads,
Our hands and our foots.

The Brightest Light

There once was a little candle named Blue. Blue lived in a box with his 44 brothers, all of them waiting for Hanukkah, when the Boy would reach into the box and place them atop the menorah for all the world to see.

But when the first night of Hanukkah came and the Boy reached into the box, he did not pick Blue. Nor did he pick him on the second night, nor on the third. And Blue was heartbroken, for he thought he would never sit atop the menorah.

"Let me tell you the one thing I have against Moses. He took us 40 years into the desert in order to bring us to the one place in the Middle East that has no oil."
–*Golda Meir*

Finally, on the eighth and final night of Hanukkah, the Boy reached into the box—and whom should he pick but Blue! And the Boy said, "Because you were so patient, I will make you the Shamash. I will light you on fire first, and then I will use your flame to kindle the rest of your brothers."

And Blue went pale and said, "Wait...what?"

The Month After Hanukkah

'Twas the month after Hanukkah,
And all through the house,
Nothing would fit me,
Not even a blouse.

The cookies I'd nibble,
The latkes I'd taste
At Hanukkah parties
Had gone to my waist.

When I got on the scales
There arose such a number!
When I walked to the store
(less a walk than a lumber),

I'd remember the marvelous
Meals I'd prepared;
The gravies and sauces
And beef nicely rared,

The wine or the egg creams,
The bread and the cheese,
And instead of "No thank you,"
It was always "Yes please."

As I dressed myself
In my husband's old shirt
And prepared once again
To do battle with dirt,

I said to myself,
As only I can,
"You can't spend the winter
Disguised as a man!"

So—away with the last
Of the sour cream dip,
Get rid of all chocolate,
Each cracker and chip.

Every last bit of food
That I like must be banished
Till all the additional
Ounces have vanished.

I won't have a cookie—
Not even a lick.
I'll chew only
On a long celery stick.

I won't have hot biscuits,
Or corn bread, or pie,
I'll munch on a carrot
And quietly cry.

I'm hungry, I'm lonesome,
And life is a bore—
But isn't that what
January is for?

Unable to giggle,
No longer a riot,
Happy New Year to all
And to all a good diet!

Christmas versus Hanukkah

1. Christmas is one day, same day every year: December 25. Jews also love December 25. It's another paid day off work. We go to movies, eat Chinese food and enjoy some Israeli dancing. Hanukkah is eight days. It starts the evening of the 24th of Kislev, whenever that falls. No one is ever sure. Jews never know until a non-Jewish friend asks when Hanukkah starts, forcing us to consult a calendar so we don't look like idiots. We all have the same calendar, provided free with a donation from the World Jewish Congress, the kosher butcher or the local Sinai Memorial Chapel (especially in Florida) or a Jewish Hebrew School.

2. Christmas is a major holiday. Hanukkah is a minor holiday with the same theme as most Jewish holidays. They tried to kill us, but we survived, so let's eat.

3. Christians get wonderful presents such as jewelry, perfume, stereos, etc. Jews get practical presents such as underwear, socks or the collected works of the Rambam, which looks impressive on the bookshelf.

4. There is only one way to spell Christmas. No one can decide how to spell Hanukkah; Chanukah, Chanukka, Channukah, Hanukah, Hannukah…

5. Christmas is a time of great pressure for husbands and boyfriends. Their partners expect special gifts. Jewish men are relieved of that burden. No one expects diamond earrings on Hanukkah.

6. Christmas brings enormous electric bills. Candles are used for Hanukkah. Not only are we spared enormous electric bills, but we also get to feel good about not contributing to the energy crisis.

7. Christmas carols are beautiful: "Silent Night," "O Come All Ye Faithful"... Hanukkah songs are about dreidels made from clay or having a party and dancing the horah. Of course, we are secretly pleased that many of the beautiful carols were composed and written by our tribal brethren. And don't Barbara Streisand and Neil Diamond sing them beautifully?

8. A home preparing for Christmas smells wonderful—the sweet smell of cookies and cakes baking. Happy people are gathered around in festive moods. A home preparing for Hanukkah smells of oil, potatoes and onions. The home, as always, is full of loud people all talking at once.

9. Women have fun baking Christmas cookies. Women burn their eyes and cut their hands grating potatoes and onions for latkes on Hanukkah. Another reminder of our suffering through the ages.

10. Parents always deliver gifts to their children on Christmas. Jewish parents have no qualms about withholding a gift on any of the eight nights.

11. The players in the Christmas story have easy to pronounce names such as Mary, Joseph and Jesus. The players in the Hanukkah story are Antiochus, Judah Maccabee and Matta whatever. No one can spell it or pronounce it. On the plus side, we can tell our friends anything and they believe we are wonderfully versed in our history.

12. Many Christians believe in the virgin birth. Jews think, "Joseph, Bubela, snap out of it. Your woman is pregnant, you didn't sleep with her, and now you want to blame God. Here's the number of my shrink."

13. In recent years, Christmas has become more and more commercialized. The same holds true for Hanukkah, even though it is a minor holiday in comparison. It makes sense. How could we market a holiday such as Yom Kippur? Forget about celebrating. Think observing. Come to synagogue, starve yourself for 27 hours, become one with your dehydrated soul, beat your chest, confess your sins—a guaranteed good time for you and your family. Tickets a mere $200 per person.

Better stick with Hanukkah!

Top 10 Hanukkah Movie Rentals

10. *Three Men and a Bubbie*
9. *A Few Hood Mentches*
8. *The Cohenheads*
7. *The Rocky Hora Picture Show*
6. *Shalom Alone*
5. *Goyz 'n the Hood*
4. *A Gefilte Fish Called Wanda*
3. *The Wizard of Oys*
2. *Who Framed Roger Rabbi?*
1. *Prelude to a Bris*

CHAPTER TWELVE
Mistletoe Miscellanea

Hurting

My friend, Rick, is a paramedic. A few years ago he answered a call about a man who had a head injury he sustained when some teenagers were throwing eggs at cars. It seems that an egg had come through the open window of the man's car as he was driving at about 45 mph. He had a large swelling on his temple. In the official report, Rick described the incident as an "egg-noggin."

Dentist

This guy goes to see his dentist because something is wrong with his mouth. After a brief examination, the dentist exclaims, "Holy Smoke! That plate I installed in your mouth about six months ago has nearly completely corroded! What on earth have you been eating?"

"Well, the only thing I can think of is this: my wife made me some asparagus about four months ago with this stuff on it—Hollandaise sauce, she called it—and doctor, I'm talkin' delicious! I've never tasted anything like it, and ever since then I've been putting it on everything—meat, fish, toast, vegetables...you name it!"

"That's probably it," replied the dentist. "Hollandaise sauce is made with lemon juice, which is acidic and highly corrosive. It seems as though I'll have to install a new plate, but made out of chrome this time."

"Why chrome?" the man asked.

"Well, everyone knows that there's no plate like chrome for the Hollandaise!"

Avon Delivery

An Avon lady was delivering the orders her customers had placed in a high-rise building downtown and was riding in the elevator. Suddenly, she had the powerful urge to fart. Since no one was in the elevator, she let it go—and it was a doozy. Of course, the elevator then stopped at the next floor, so she quickly used some Avon pine-scented spray to cover up the smell before the doors opened.

A man entered the elevator and immediately made a face. "Holy cow! What's that smell?"

"I don't know, sir. I don't smell anything. What does it smell like to you?"

"Like someone crapped a Christmas tree."

Overrun

Three buildings in town were overrun by squirrels: the town hall, the hardware store and the church. The town hall brought in some cats. But after they tore up all the files, the mayor got rid of the predators, and soon the squirrels were back. The hardware store humanely trapped the squirrels and set them free outside town. But three days later, the squirrels were back. Only the church came up with an effective solution. They baptized the squirrels and made them members. Now they see them only on Christmas and Easter.

Name That Christmas Carol: A Quiz

The following are re-wordings of Christmas carol titles and lines. See how many you can get!

1. Quadruped with crimson proboscis
2. 5:00 pm to 6:00 am without noise
3. Miniscule hamlet in the Middle East
4. Ancient benevolent despot
5. Adorn the vestibule
6. Exuberance directed to the planet
7. Listen! Aerial spirits harmonizing
8. Monarchial trio
9. Yonder in a feed trough
10. Assemble, everyone who believes
11. Hallowed post meridian
12. It's fixin' to appear extremely similar to December 25th
13. Tin tintinnabulums
14. A dozen 24-hour Yule periods
15. Befell during the transparent bewitching hour
16. Homo sapiens of crystallized vapor
17. I merely desire a pair of incisors

18. I spied my maternal parent osculating a fat man in red

19. Perambulating in a December solstice fantasy land

20. Aloft on the acme of the abode

21. Slumber in ethereal quiet...

22. Hey there! The announcing celestial beings carol...

23. O greetings of ease and happiness...

24. On commencement of Yuletide my honey bestowed upon me...

25. Decorate the passage with branches of evergreen sprigs...

26. Then upon a misty night prior to Christ's birthday...

27. Ooh, celestial body of marvel, celestial body of darkness...

28. With a vegetable stem smoker and a clothes fastening snout...

29. It's a fluff-ball sphere in the cold season...

30. Come on, come on, come on, let's get moving...

31. O scared darkness, the asterisks are brilliantly shimmering...

32. I'm having fantasies of a colorless December 25th...

33. Small children with their optical aids entirely illuminated...

34. Loyal buddies who are important to us collect closely to us again...

35. Boppin' while circling the tannenbaum...

36. Royalty of royalties, always and always...

37. O approach, y'all devoted, happy and victorious...

38. Urban walkways, congested walkways, trimmed in a festive manner...

39. Ah, the atmospheric condition beyond is terrific...

40. Percussion instruments jingle, are you harking...

41. Remarked the evening breeze to the tiny sheep...

42. Wishing your waking hours be gleeful and dazzling...

43. Harmony on the planet, kindness to Homo sapiens...

44. Hop in the sack, hide your noggin, since the fat man comes this evening...

45. Ourselves bid yourselves a joyous Noel and a cheerful neoteric 365 days...

ANSWERS:

1. "Rudolph the Red-nosed Reindeer"

2. "Silent Night"

3. "O Little Town of Bethlehem"

4. "Good King Wenceslas"
   (or "Jolly Old St. Nicholas")

5. "Deck the Halls"

6. "Joy to the World"

7. "Hark! The Herald Angels Sing"

8. "We Three Kings"

9. "Away in a Manger"

10. "O Come All Ye Faithful"

11. "O Holy Night"

12. "It's Beginning to Look a Lot Like Christmas"

13. "Silver Bells"

14. "The Twelve Days of Christmas"

15. "It Came Upon the Midnight Clear"

16. "Frosty the Snowman"

17. "All I Want for Christmas Is My Two Front Teeth"

18. "I Saw Mommy Kissing Santa Claus"

19. "Walking in a Winter Wonderland"

20. "Up on the Housetop"

21. Sleep in heavenly peace... "Silent Night"

22. Hark! the herald angels sing... "Hark! The Herald Angels Sing"

23. O tidings of comfort and joy... "God Rest Ye Merry, Gentlemen"

24. On the first day of Christmas, my true love gave to me... "The Twelve Days of Christmas"

25. Deck the halls with boughs of holly... "Deck the Halls"

26. Then one foggy Christmas Eve... "Rudolph the Red-nosed Reindeer"

27. O-oh star of wonder, star of night... "We Three Kings"

28. With a corncob pipe and a button nose... "Frosty the Snowman"

29. It's a marshmallow world in the winter... "It's a Marshmallow World"

30. Giddyap, giddyap, giddyap, let's go... "Sleigh Ride"

31. O Holy night, the stars are brightly shining... "O Holy Night"

32. I'm dreaming of a white Christmas... "White Christmas"

33. Tiny tots with their eyes all aglow... "The Christmas Song"

34. Faithful friends who are dear to us, gather near to us once more... "Have Yourself a Merry Little Christmas"

35. Rockin' around the Christmas tree... "Rockin' Around the Christmas Tree"

36. King of Kings, forever and ever... "Hallelujah" chorus from "The Messiah"

37. Oh come, all ye faithful, joyful and triumphant... "Oh Come All Ye Faithful"

38. City sidewalks, busy sidewalks, dressed in holiday style... "Silver Bells"

39. Oh, the weather outside is frightful... "Let It Snow"

40. Sleigh bells ring, are you listening...
    "Walking in a Winter Wonderland"

41. Said the night wind to the little lamb...
    "Do You Hear What I Hear"

42. May your days be merry and bright...
    "White Christmas"

43. Peace on Earth, goodwill toward men...
    "I Heard the Bells on Christmas Day"

44. Jump in bed, cover up your head, 'cause
    Santa Claus comes tonight...
    "Here Comes Santa Claus"

45. We wish you a merry Christmas, and
    a happy New Year...
    "We Wish You a Merry Christmas"

RESULTS:

34–45 Correct: You don't need any Yuletide spirit!

21–33 Correct: You could use something in
               your stocking!

0–20 Correct: Are you the Grinch?!

Christmas Thoughts

- I wanna tell you what kind of luck I've got.
  If this year I cornered the mistletoe market,
  they'd postpone Christmas.

- Christmas: when you exchange hellos with
  strangers and good buys with friends.

- Christmas is the time when people put so
  many bulbs on the outside of their houses,

you don't know if they're celebrating the birth of Jesus or General Electric.

- Christmas in L.A. is always interesting…seeing carolers dressed in Bermuda shorts, groping their way through the smog, singing, "It came upon the midnight clear."
- If Christmas, Father's Day and birthdays did not exist, then aftershave too, might not exist.
- Christmas: the time when everyone gets Santa-mental.
- I know, I know. I know that people say, "It's the thought that counts, not the gift," but couldn't people think a little bigger?
- Santa Claus is a jolly fellow! Imagine all that driving and still being able to say, "Ho! Ho! Ho!
- Every year, Christmas becomes less a birthday and more a clearance sale.
- Christmas is in my heart twelve months a year, and thanks to credit cards, it's on my Visa statement twelve months a year also.
- I bought my friend some gift wrap for Christmas. I took it to the gift-wrap counter and told them to wrap it, but in different paper, so he'd know when to stop unwrapping.
- When I was young, we were poor. We didn't have a Christmas tree. We had a Christmas stump.
- Christmas is a time when people get emotional over family ties, particularly if they have to wear them.

- It was so cold on Christmas Eve at the North Pole that Santa had to jump-start three of his reindeer.

- I hope Santa brings me that mistletoe belt I asked for!

- I think that Santa is very jolly because he knows where all the bad girls live.

- No one in the history of the world has ever purchased a fruitcake for themselves.

- No parent in their right mind would give a six-year-old a drum set; therefore, Santa exists.

- The three stages of man: 1) he believes in Santa Claus; 2) he doesn't believe in Santa Claus; 3) he is Santa Claus.

- We were so poor in our house when I was young, that on Christmas morning, if you didn't wake up with a hard-on, you had f*ck all to play with.

- I wanted my step-daughter to play with the rabbit I bought her for Christmas, but her mother said that a sex toy was not an appropriate gift for an eight-year-old.

- I'm dreaming of a white Christmas—not because I like snow or anything, I'm just a racist.

- I've been bad a few times this year, but it was worth it.

- I once wanted to become an atheist, but I gave up. They have no holidays.

- I've just got my son a flattened piece of cardboard for Christmas. Although what he wants with an ex-box, I'll never know.

- Only six shopping days until Christmas! Or if you're a bloke, only five and a half days until you start your Christmas shopping.

- The first present I opened this Christmas was a penknife. I was so excited, I used it to cut open all my other presents. Shame about the puppy.

- When I was a kid, our Christmases were very poor. We couldn't afford tinsel. We had to wait for grandpa to sneeze.

- I got a sweater for Christmas. I was hoping for a screamer or a moaner.

- My girlfriend told me she was hoping for a white Christmas, so I spunked in her eyes.

- Is that snow outside, or did Lindsay Lohan just sneeze?

- Nothing like a dysfunctional family trying to function for the holidays.

- Just a reminder in these tough economic times that instead of spending five dollars on my Christmas card, you could just give me five dollars.

- I always get my loved ones petrol-soaked fake moustaches for Christmas. It's such a joy to watch their faces light up!

Christmas Quotes

Santa Claus? You have to look very carefully at a man like this. He comes but once a year? Down the chimney? And in my sock?

—Professor Irwin Corey

I never believed in Santa Claus because I knew no white man would be coming into my neighborhood after dark.

—Dick Gregory

I must say, when the doorman where I live puts up the Christmas tree in the lobby, he has the same friendly smile for those who have remembered him at Christmas and for those who have not. Except that when he trims the tree, if you have not, there you are on the tree hanging in effigy.

—Selma Diamond

New Year's Eve, when auld acquaintances be forgot. Unless, of course, those tests come back positive.

—Jay Leno

"Have you been a good boy all year?" Damn him! Damn Santa Claus—has anybody ever been a good boy all year? "He's making a list, checking it twice. He's gonna find out who's naughty or nice." Who the hell did he think he was, J. Edgar Hoover?

—Allan Sherman

I remember a Christmas years ago when my son was a kid. I bought him a tank. It was about a hundred dollars, a lot of money in those days. It was the kind of tank you could actually get inside and ride. Instead, he played in the box it came in. It taught me a valuable lesson. Next year he got a box, and I got a hundred dollars worth of scotch.

–Unknown

I wanted our street to have the prettiest Christmas decorations in the neighborhood, so I strung colored balls from house to house, all the way down the block. And I did all the electrical wiring myself. If you'd like further information, just drive down Moorpark Street in North Hollywood. We're the third pile of ashes from the corner.

–Bob Hope

I had a big New Year's Eve—they tell me. But New Year's Eve is a lot of fun. We had a big party. We didn't like our furniture anyway. It was 18th-century Provincial. Now it's 20th-century splinters. I invited Les Brown and had the band over. We didn't like our neighbors either. I invited the brass section, too. We don't even like ourselves.

–Bob Hope

I once bought my kids a set of batteries for Christmas with a note on it saying, toys not included.

–Bernard Manning

I was Christmas shopping and ran into a guy on the street. I noticed his watch and said that it runs slow. He said, "So does the guy I stole it from."

—David Letterman

The one thing women don't want to find in their stockings on Christmas morning is their husband.

—Joan Rivers

Today, President Obama announced that he's giving all federal employees Christmas Eve off. And when Joe Biden heard that he was like, "But not Santa, right?"

—Jimmy Fallon

According to a new poll, most Americans think Santa Claus is a Democrat—which is really odd because when I think of a fat, old white man who hires unskilled labor, I think Republican.

—Conan O'Brien

I stopped believing in Santa Claus when my mother took me to see him in a department store, and he asked for my autograph.

—Shirley Temple

Christmas is just around the corner. It's just under two weeks away, and today Santa released 10 years of tax returns.

—David Letterman

The Obamas have decorated the White House with 54 Christmas trees. It's all part of their "For the last time, we're not Muslim" campaign.

–*Conan O'Brien*

The Mayans have predicted the world is supposed to end on December 21. If the world doesn't end on December 21, you can bet the next day the malls will be overrun with Mayans trying to buy last-minute gifts.

–*Jay Leno*

I was thinking about Santa Claus. When you really think about it, this has to be the biggest, most elaborate prank in the history of the world. It's like we're all in on a huge joke we're playing on kids. And eventually they figure it out and they start lying to their kids, too.

–*Jimmy Kimmel*

The Rockefeller Center's Christmas tree is being put in place this afternoon. They bring it in and hoist it with a crane and steel cables. It's the same way they get Chris Christie into his pants.

–*David Letterman*

"Did you hear about the al-Qaeda Christmas party? No dancing or music, but the fastest game of pass the parcel you've ever seen."

–*Omid Djalili*

The wife of a man who never learned the difference between a brassiere and a brazier was granted a divorce today on two counts. First because when she wanted underwear for Christmas he gave her two big rusty tins with holes in, and second because of the way he kept trying to roast his chestnuts.

–Ronnie Barker

Then they start decorating the tree with a beautiful array of Christmas lights and on the very top they put a tiny little Mayor Bloomberg. In fact, it actually is Mayor Bloomberg.

–David Letterman

Christmas is less than two weeks away. I do most of my shopping online. But I hire someone to honk and scream obscenities at me while I'm doing it so I get the whole holiday shopping experience.

–Jimmy Kimmel

Roses are reddish,
Violets are bluish,
If it weren't for Christmas,
We'd all be Jewish.

–Benny Hill

Santa Claus has the right idea—visit people only once a year.

–Victor Borge

The fact of the matter is, Santa isn't a Democrat or a Republican. In fact, Santa isn't even an American. I have news for you. The real Santa is Chinese. You think elves are the ones making that plastic crap we give our kids? No. Chinese people are.

–Jimmy Kimmel

The other night they had that "Christmas in Washington" holiday special. And you know, people in Washington, right away the bickering started. Lou Dobbs accused Santa of using illegal immigrant labor. Rush Limbaugh said the gifts were part of some kind of socialist give-away program. The AFL-CIO claims that Santa underpays his elves, and of course, since it's Washington, you're not going to find three wise men and a virgin. So the whole thing was pretty much a disaster.

–Jay Leno

Christmas at my house is always at least six or seven times more pleasant than anywhere else. We start drinking early. And while everyone else is seeing only one Santa Claus, we'll be seeing six or seven.

–W.C. Fields

A survey found that 66 million Americans haven't started their holiday shopping. Which means they only have 14 more days to find out which gas station near their house sells Chili's gift cards.

–Jimmy Fallon

Christmas and the New Year are actually two holidays. So there is a plural, which in the English language, necessitates the use of "s." I suppose you could say "Merry Christmas and happy New Year," but you probably have sh*t to do.

—Jon Stewart, on Bill O'Reilly's objection to "Happy Holidays"

According to a new CBS poll, 33 percent of Americans say they won't have enough money to cover their holiday spending. I believe these people are called Congress.

—Jay Leno

This year, the Treasury Department is holding its annual holiday party inside something called the cash room. You know what that is in Washington, the cash room? That's a big room where the Treasury Department holds all its cash it has on hand. Of course, these days it's empty, so plenty more room to party.

—Jay Leno

You folks feeling the economic pinch? Are you a little fed up with the economic news? It's bad. The department stores, this holiday season, no Santa Claus. They're laying off department-store Santa Clauses. So more bad news for John McCain.

—David Letterman

Americans say they are planning to do a lot of their holiday shopping this year at warehouse stores like Costco. Because, folks, nothing says Merry Christmas like 90 rolls of toilet paper.

–Conan O'Brien

Christmas begins about the first of December with an office party and ends when you finally realize what you spent, around April 15 of the next year.

–P.J. O'Rourke, Modern Manners

There are a lot of holiday parties coming up at the White House. Obama is getting ready to host the administration's first Hanukkah party tomorrow. Kind of an embarrassing moment, though. Today, after they lit the menorah, Biden blew it out and made a wish.

–Jimmy Fallon

One of the holiday decorations at the White House is a 400-pound gingerbread house. Isn't that nice? And in front of that is a 400-pound gingerbread "foreclosed" sign.

–Conan O'Brien

President Obama went Christmas shopping at Best Buy in Virginia this week. He had to go to Best Buy because he's not allowed to go to Walmart, because China said, "You can't buy any more stuff from us until you pay off what you already owe us."

–Jay Leno

President Obama bought about $200 worth of Christmas presents at Best Buy. Then it got awkward when he asked the Geek Squad if they fix economies.

–Jimmy Fallon

As they do every year, al-Qaeda has threatened to disrupt and ruin Christmas. You know, we already have a group that disrupts and ruins Christmas every year. They're called relatives.

–Jay Leno

Vice President Joe Biden just mailed his family Christmas card, which is signed with his dog Champ's paw print. The weird thing is, Biden actually does that with all his important documents.

–Jimmy Fallon

I wrapped my Christmas presents early this year, but I used the wrong paper. The paper I used said "Happy Birthday" on it. I didn't want to waste it, so I just wrote "Jesus" on it.

–Demetri Martin

Roger Johnson

Roger Johnson is a man of the world. He has traveled from Timbuktu to Dildo, Newfoundland, seeking out new experiences and adventures along the way. On top of being a traveler, Roger Johnson is also a writer who has a passion for a good punch line. Jokes are his *raison-d'être*. Roger Johnson is a member of MENSA, the Water Buffalo Bowling Team out of Minnesota, the Bilderberg Club, the Bohemian Club and sometimes has time to visit with the Freemasons.